CREWE ALEXANDRA

THE OFFICIAL REVIEW 2003-04

Norwich's Robert Green makes
a mess of Dean Ashton's shot in
the final game of the 2003/04
season, as Jonah looks poised
to make sure.

CREWE ALEXANDRA

THE OFFICIAL REVIEW 2003-04

A Season of Two Halves

by Rob Wilson and Andy Wilkinson
Photography by Peter Warburton

breedon **books**
PUBLISHING

First published in Great Britain in 2004 by
The Breedon Books Publishing Company Limited
Breedon House, 3 The Parker Centre,
Derby, DE21 4SZ.

Photography Acknowledgements

Peter Warburton
Tim Jervis
Keith Slater
Laurie Rampling
Andrea Tennant
Andy Pack
Rich Walker
Action Images
Empics
www.bradfordcityfc.co.uk
www.saddlers.co.uk

ISBN 1 85983 430 2

Printed and bound by Scotprint, Haddington, Scotland.

Contents

Foreword by Dario Gradi   6

The Summer Months   8

Pre-Season Results   9

August Review   10

September Review   24

October Review   36

November Review   50

December Review   62

January Review   76

February Review   86

March Review   94

April Review   110

May Review   122

Looking Forward – A Supporter's View   128

Player Profiles   132

Youth Cup Action   166

Reaseheath Training Ground   172

Opposition Preview   175

Supporters' Roll of Honour   187

Foreword

by Dario Gradi

Having just seen Bristol City lose yet again in the play-offs for the right to play in the First Division after around six years in Division Two, I love to look back on the season before last as a superb achievement. To bounce back after only one year was special. In many ways to stay up last season was also a decent achievement especially as the bookies had us as favourites to go down. Slowly but surely the smaller clubs are being replaced by the bigger ones.

Last year Wimbledon and Walsall, two of the least supported clubs, went down with Bradford City, who attract considerably bigger crowds. They were replaced by Plymouth Argyle, QPR and Brighton, of which only Brighton have a tough time attracting over 6,000, meaning they will probably be one of the favourites for relegation.

Probably the only other clubs still in the league with gates under 10,000 are Gillingham, Rotherham and of course us. Any three from that four then? Well there is often a side that underachieves, as perhaps Bradford have done this season, so any three from five maybe.

Can we do better? Well I watched the play-offs and couldn't help thinking how well we were doing to be playing in the same league as West Ham, Ipswich, Sunderland and Crystal Palace. Then I thought we had done better than that by taking four points off Sunderland and three off Crystal Palace and Ipswich. To do that we must have some talented players. Our performance in Division Two would also support that theory.

So what is required? Firstly I think the players must reach a higher level of consistency and also a higher level of performance. Some have found it harder this season to shine and I think a lot of that is down to the fact that there are bigger, stronger, better athletes playing in Division One. Go up to the Premier League and that is definitely the case! The ability to impose yourself physically on your opponent can only improve confidence. Therefore, once again, the players are working hard during the summer to improve physically. They were only off for one week and then they were back at it. No football, just mainly strengthening work. I don't think any other club will have matched our players for work during the close season. Credit for this must go to fitness coach Andy Franks and weightlifting expert Barry Beasley, who end up working all year round.

Our work to improve facilities continues. The pitch at the stadium will be better than ever this season as we ended the season with a fair amount of grass on it. The same can be said of the training pitches, and this summer we have installed an irrigation system and the surface has been improved by sand splitting, which will help with drainage.

During the summer we have worked on the individual progress of the players as well as teamwork. I also have some ideas about changing the shape of the team and hope that it might help to make a difference. Most important though is the improvement in the players we already have. We are not looking for new skills from them, only for them to improve those skills in the game and make a real difference. Good examples might be Ben Rix and David Vaughan, who imposed themselves more in games in Division Two than Division One. They are both very talented, skilful footballers who have benefited from the strength programme this summer. I think all the players have it in them to improve and if we can press the right buttons they will.

I need to find two or three players to strengthen the side. Last season Dean Ashton and Steve Jones didn't have the necessary support or competition. Paul Edwards, Michael Higdon, Luke Varney or perhaps James Robinson will push for a challenge this season but I can't rely on that. The season before last we had Rob Hulse and Rodney Jack. Nor do we get enough goals from elsewhere. So are we going to get more goals from Kenny Lunt, Neil Sorvel, Justin Cochrane, David Vaughan, Ben Rix and so on, or do we need someone with a better goal-scoring record? If so, can we afford him?

The death of Telford United serves once more to illustrate the importance of living within your means. I'm sure their Chairman and benefactor had the best intentions in mind but while I am no financial expert I'm sure you don't go bankrupt overnight. In the end his overspending has put Telford out of business. Not a situation our directors would allow.

So we will prepare for another season in Division One ready to fight the odds. Our willingness to work hard will always give us a chance. Whether we can reach the top half of the league is uncertain. I will not be surprised if we do and I suppose I will not be surprised if we don't, but it is possible and that is what drives us on.

What is for certain is that we will still be in business at the end of the season.

DARIO GRADI: FACTFILE

Name: Dario Gradi MBE

Born: 8 July 1941 in Milan, Italy

Playing Career:
Fulham Juniors
Tooting and Mitcham
Sutton United

Managerial Career:
Chelsea Assistant Coach
1971

Sutton United Manager
1976/77

Derby County Assistant Manager
1977/78

Wimbledon Manager
1978–81

Crystal Palace Manager
1981

Leyton Orient Youth Team Coach
1981–83

Crewe Alexandra Manager
June 1983–present

Honours:
Promotion from old Fourth Division
1989

Promotion from Third Division
1994

Promotion from Second Division –
play-off winners 1997

Awarded MBE in January 1998

Milestone of 1,000 games in November
2001

Promotion from Second Division
2002

PFA Special Merit Award in April 2004

The Summer Months

Shaun and Macca enjoy their day with their children.

One of the hottest summers on record saw three former favourites leave the Alexandra Stadium and two former greats finally receive the send-off they deserved for over 10 years of service.

Dave Walton moved on to Derby County on a free transfer. The former Shrewsbury Town and Sheffield United defender elected not to sign a new contract at Crewe and moved on after six years and 169 appearances. That total would have been even greater if it wasn't for the number of injuries he suffered during his spell with us.

The club's record signing, Rodney Jack, also rejected the chance of a new deal at Gresty Road and decided to move to newly promoted Rushden and Diamonds once his contract had expired with us. He teamed up with another Crewe favourite, Marcus Bignot, at Nene Park and proved a success in Division Two. The St Vincent International scored 42 goals in 196 appearances for Crewe Alexandra during a period of five years.

Rob Hulse was different. With a year of his contract still to run, the Crewe-born forward felt he owed the club some return on their investment and in the interests of both parties, Hulse was sold to West Bromwich Albion for a fee rising to £1 million depending on appearances.

Hulse's move to the Hawthorns meant Crewe entered the First Division without their top scorer from the previous season. The hardworking forward had plundered 27 goals in the Second Division and unsurprisingly Cardiff City, Norwich City, Wigan Athletic and Millwall all chased his signature once Dario made it known that Rob wouldn't be staying at his home club. Saying that, West Brom was always his first choice.

The relatively unknown midfielder Justin Cochrane proved to be a shrewd acquisition when he impressed in a couple of trial games and then on our pre-season trip to Portugal. Although another midfielder was hardly high on the list of the manager's priorities, Cochrane's determination to return to the professional game was quite evident. After being released by Queens Park Rangers, the combative midfielder had been spotted by a Crewe scout playing for Hayes in the Ryman League Premier Division.

Dario Gradi chats to Liverpool boss Gerard Houllier before our pre-season friendly.

The 21-year-old Londoner made an immediate impact with a man-of-the-match performance against Everton in pre-season, and he would become a integral member of the first-team squad. When he was missing due to injury or suspension we certainly missed his competitiveness.

Yorkshireman Adie Moses proved a reliable replacement for Dave Walton but, like his predecessor, suffered injury-wise in his first season with us. Moses, who had previously played for Barnsley in the Premiership, arrived from financially troubled Huddersfield Town on a free transfer. Money was hardly an issue for him when negotiating his contract and his experience and presence became a key factor at Reaseheath and in the dressing room.

Dario Gradi could not have asked for a better pre-season campaign. Convincing away victories over near neighbours Port Vale (4–1) and Tranmere Rovers (5–0) were surpassed by our performances against Liverpool and most notably Everton in the Shaun Smith/Steve Macauley testimonials.

Both Merseyside clubs honoured a long-standing agreement to bring strong squads to the Alexandra Stadium and the people of Crewe were delighted to see the likes of Michael Owen, Steven Gerrard, Duncan Ferguson and Wayne Rooney strut their stuff in front of a combined gate of nearly 18,000.

A rare headed goal from Michael Owen cancelled out David Vaughan's opener in the first game while goals from Dean Ashton and Ben Rix saw us record a 2–0 win over David Moyes's side.

The high-profile matches were a fitting tribute to Smith and Macauley, who will best be remembered for the influential part they played in helping the club to promotion in 1997.

Other pre-season friendlies against Altrincham, Stafford, Kidsgrove Athletic, Congleton and Nantwich were not as glamorous but gave a number of youngsters and trialists an opportunity to stake a claim to a place in the first-team squad.

August Review

John Bowler and Dario Gradi receive the freedom of the Borough.

After a terrific pre-season campaign which saw some great results over Everton, Tranmere Rovers, Port Vale and Liverpool, everyone was looking forward to the new 2003–04 campaign and another chance for Dario Gradi's young squad to take the First Division by surprise.

The winning mentality that was so well established during our promotion from the Second Division went a long way towards rebuilding the confidence of the players. A year in the lower league certainly helped the development of the younger and inexperienced players and despite the loss of Rodney Jack, Rob Hulse and Dave Walton, there was still great optimism around the training ground, despite the fact that every critic in the land had us down as certs for relegation!

The possibility of surpassing the football club's highest ever placing of 11th became a realistic target and there was even a hint of a push for the play-off places until injuries finally began to take their toll going into the New Year. Dario said before a ball was even kicked:

Top Scorer Rob Hulse was sold to West Bromwich Albion for £1 million in July.

'We think we will be alright this season but you can never tell what will happen because luck does play its part, especially with injuries. I would like to add a couple of players because we need a bit of cover in certain positions.

People write us off but we have survived and held our own before in the First Division and we don't take much notice of those who predict positions in the newspapers. It is just up to the players to prove it.'

The opening game of the season at a deserted Selhurst Park certainly bought us back down to earth with a bump!

It had begun so well, too, with captain Dave Brammer (via a wicked deflection) opening our goal-scoring account for the season against Wimbledon in sweltering conditions. But stunning individual goals from Patrick Agyemang, Alex Tapp and Nigel Reo-Coker continued our dismal run of performance at this particular ground. In fact, we had never won at Selhurst Park until we defeated the landlords Crystal Palace in early December, ironically by the same scoreline.

The opening month of the season improved with a fairly comfortable victory over Wrexham in the Carling Cup and then an excellent 1–0 win over promotion candidates Ipswich Town. The match winner on a memorable afternoon was Kenny Lunt, who curled home one of his trademark free-kicks.

Only a last-ditch header from Noel Whelan prevented us from grabbing our first away win of the campaign at the New Den. Another home victory, this time over Colin Lee's Walsall side, arrived just three days later with Steve Jones toe-poking home the only goal of the game.

A busy month ended with a narrow 1–0 defeat at Burnley. Midfielder Richard Chaplow scored the only goal of a tight affair at Turf Moor.

August was a month of ups and downs, and saw Crewe nicely positioned in 13th place on seven points. Already a faint pattern was beginning to be established, with Crewe becoming increasingly difficult to beat at home, but finding it harder to pick up points on the road. It was a complete reverse of the previous season when we won a record 14 times on our travels.

Nigerian defender Efe Sodje left the club to join Third Division Huddersfield Town after Adie Moses made the reverse switch to Gresty Road earlier in the summer.

Dario also made Stockport County's left-back Anthony Tonkin his number one priority and publicly declared his interest in Shrewsbury Town's livewire Luke Rodgers. Jimmy Quinn quickly priced his sought-after striker out of a potential move by putting a £1 million price tag on his head. Tonkin was another story and before the month had elapsed he had handed in a written transfer request to an unhappy Carlton Palmer.

Away from football, Chairman John Bowler and Dario Gradi were awarded the freedom of Crewe and Nantwich Borough for their services to the community.

Saturday 9 August 2003 – 3pm – Selhurst Park – Att: 1,145

Wimbledon 3   Crewe Alexandra 1

Agyemang 15
Tapp 54
Reo-Coker 62

Brammer 8

Wimbledon

1	Steve Banks
3	Peter Hawkins
6	Darren Holloway
11	Patrick Agyemang
17	Adam Nowland
19	Ben Chorley
20	Mikele Leigertwood
23	Alex Tapp
24	Jermaine Darlington
26	Nigel Reo-Coker
27	Michael Gordon

Substitutes

10	Dean Holdsworth (Agyemang 84)
13	Paul Heald
15	Albert Jarrett
22	Rob Gier
28	Malvin Kamara (Gordon 88)

Referee

Mr K. Hill (Royston)

Crewe Alexandra

1	Clayton Ince
2	David Wright
4	Kenny Lunt
5	Adie Moses
6	Stephen Foster
8	Dave Brammer
9	Steve Jones
11	David Vaughan
14	Ben Rix
17	James Robinson
19	Justin Cochrane

Substitutes

12	Lee Bell (Cochrane 85)
13	Ademole Bankole
15	Luke Varney (Robinson 74)
18	Chris McCready (Moses 79)
28	Jonathan Walters

MATCH REPORT

In sweltering conditions in front of a sparse crowd at Selhurst Park, Crewe Alexandra made their return to the First Division in disappointing fashion with a 3–1 defeat against pre-season relegation favourites Wimbledon.

Before such a disappointing crowd, which was roughly split 50/50 between Crewe fans and Wimbledon supporters, it was the Alex who made a flying start as Dave Brammer's deflected effort gave the Railwaymen a 1–0 lead, but three excellent goals from the impressive young Dons gave Stuart Murdoch's side all three points on the opening day of the season.

Dario Gradi handed summer signings Adie Moses and Justin Cochrane their debuts, while young Academy graduate James Robinson made his first start for the club up front in place of the injured Dean Ashton, and things started well with Brammer's eighth-minute strike.

After cutting in from the left, and just a few yards outside the box, Brammer let fly with a shot which, from the main stand, looked like a screamer into the top corner, although video replays later showed it took a wicked deflection off Wimbledon defender Mikele Leigertwood before evading the clutches of goalkeeper Steve Banks.

That was the high spot for the Alex, and the lead lasted just seven minutes before the home side found themselves on level terms.

Patrick Agyemang brought his side level when a slip by Moses allowed him to run through the Crewe defence before finishing coolly past Clayton Ince into the bottom corner to top an excellent solo move.

The conditions got even hotter in the second half and although the Alex had their chances, the players seemed to wilt a little in the conditions and lost to two Wimbledon

Dario's Comments

'I have never been involved in a game at home or abroad played in that heat and it made it a strange match and very difficult for the players. We defended poorly, particularly for the first goal, but the others came out of the blue and I wouldn't expect Wimbledon to score many more like that all season.'

Stuart Murdoch's Comments

'Nigel Reo-Coker looked amazing and charged up and down the pitch. People have said that both Crewe and ourselves are going down, but there are 45 games to play. We both still have decent players and have youth on our side.'

The Sun

Wimbledon collected all three points on merit – a fact readily conceded by former Dons manager Dario Gradi, starting his 21st season in charge of Crewe. How anyone could play in the heat was astonishing, but the players deserved their ovation at the end.

The Sentinel

Crewe barely got out of third gear after being handed the best possible start when skipper Dave Brammer drove into the far corner superbly after skipping in from the left. Brammer and debutant Justin Cochrane tried hard to get the Alex into the game, but the hosts had the edge in the middle of the park with the tireless work of Reo-Coker.

wonder strikes. First, on 54 minutes full-back Alex Tapp scored the goal of his life when he drifted in from the right before cracking a left-footed screamer into the top corner of Ince's goal, and then just after the hour mark the game was over when Nigel Reo-Coker thumped another left-footed shot home from outside the area after a quick Wimbledon counter-attack.

It was a disappointing start to the season for sure, but the untimely deaths of former Blackburn manager Ray Harford and Manchester United youngster Jimmy Davis on the morning of the game really put football into perspective that day.

David Wright, sporting a new skinhead, halts Patrick Agyemang in his tracks.

Crewe celebrate Dave Brammer's deflected opener at a deserted Wimbledon.

Tuesday 12 August 2003 – 7.45pm – Gresty Road – Att: 3,152

Crewe Alexandra 2 Wrexham 0

Ashton 54 (pen)
S. Jones 88

Crewe Alexandra

1	Clayton Ince
2	David Wright
4	Kenny Lunt
5	Adie Moses
6	Stephen Foster
8	Dave Brammer
9	Steve Jones
10	Dean Ashton
11	David Vaughan
14	Ben Rix
19	Justin Cochrane

Substitutes

12	Lee Bell
13	Ademole Bankole
15	Luke Varney
17	James Robinson
18	Chris McCready (Ashton 76)

Referee

Mr T. Parkes (Birmingham)

Wrexham

1	Andy Dibble
2	Jim Whitley
5	Brian Carey
6	Dennis Lawrence
7	Carlos Edwards
8	Lee Jones
10	Darren Ferguson
11	Chris Llewellyn
14	Paul Edwards
18	Shaun Pejic
19	Stephen Thomas

Substitutes

3	Shaun Holmes
13	Paul Whitfield
15	Craig Morgan
16	Matty Crowell (Thomas 84)
23	Hector Sam (Jones 45)

MATCH REPORT

Crewe claimed their first victory of the new season as Dean Ashton marked his return to the side from injury with his first goal of the campaign and Steve Jones bagged a late strike to knock Second Division Wrexham out of the Carling Cup.

Just three days after the disappointing defeat at Wimbledon the Alex made hard work of the first half against Denis Smith's well-organised side but produced a much better second-half display to book a second-round clash at Premiership club Leicester City.

Ashton had already gone close from a Dave Brammer cross just after the half time interval when, on 52 minutes, he was handed a much easier chance to score when referee Trevor Parkes awarded the Alex a penalty following Darren Ferguson's rash challenge on Ben Rix just inside the box. Ashton sent Wrexham keeper Andy Dibble the wrong way from the spot and Crewe never looked back.

The Alex were relentless as they looked to make the game safe and although Red Dragons substitute Hector Sam had his chances to equalise, one of which rattled Clayton Ince's crossbar, there was only going to be one winner and that was the Railwaymen.

However, despite creating several chances, the home fans were made to wait until two minutes from time to celebrate another goal as Jones cleverly collected a long ball from Stephen Foster and protected the ball with his body before swivelling and expertly chipping a shot over the advancing Dibble to make it 2–0. The visitors then pressed the self-destruct button as frustration boiled over into anger, and manager Smith was sent from the dug-out, to be quickly followed into the dressing rooms by defender Brian Carey, who was dismissed for a professional foul on livewire Jones in the final minute.

Dario's Comments
'I thought it was a decent performance because we stuck at it. We have certainly played better than this but we were relentless in the end. By half time I believe we were in control of the game and in control of the midfield. We won the battle in the midfield and kept winning possession.'

Denis Smith's Comments
'I know it's all about results, but we were the better team and we lost the game. But you can't beat the officials if they were as bad as they were tonight. For the penalty the ball was a foot outside and anyway it should not have been a penalty because Darren Ferguson won the ball. So if you are asking if the referee had a good game then the answer is no.'

The Sentinel
The Alex moved into the second round of the Carling Cup thanks to a rousing second-half display against a bad-tempered Wrexham side. After a lacklustre first-half display Dean Ashton's penalty and a well-deserved goal by Steve Jones were enough to send Dario Gradi's side through.

The Sun
Wrexham boss Denis Smith was sent off and was quickly followed by Brian Carey in a bad-tempered match at Gresty Road. Smith's continual arguing with the officials saw him sent from the dug-out and Carey walked for a professional foul as Crewe won 2–0 with goals by Ashton and Jones.

Captain Dave Brammer led Crewe to victory over his previous club Wrexham.

Crewe Alexandra 1 Ipswich Town 0

Lunt 69

Crewe Alexandra

1 Clayton Ince
2 David Wright
4 Kenny Lunt
5 Adie Moses
6 Stephen Foster
8 Dave Brammer
9 Steve Jones
10 Dean Ashton
14 Ben Rix
18 Chris McCready
19 Justin Cochrane

Substitutes

12 Lee Bell (Rix 89)
13 Ademole Bankole
15 Luke Varney
20 Allan Smart
28 Jonathan Walters

Referee

Mr R. Pearson (Peterlee)

Ipswich Town

1 Kelvin Davis
2 Fabian Wilnis
3 Chris Makin
5 Drissa Diallo
7 Jim Magilton
8 Tommy Miller
12 Richard Naylor
16 Marcus Bent
18 Darren Bent
23 George Santos
30 Martijn Reuser

Substitutes

9 Pablo Gonzalez Counago
   (Reuser 45)
11 Jermaine Wright (Santos 45)
14 Matthew Richards
17 Dean Bowditch
35 Lewis Price

MATCH REPORT

The ever-reliable Kenny Lunt took all the plaudits as the Alex collected their first three points of the season to stun promotion hopefuls Ipswich Town at the Alexandra Stadium.

Lunt's second-half free kick might have been the only goal of the game but that hardly told the full story as both sides created numerous chances with only a combination of poor finishing and wonderful goalkeeping from both Clayton Ince and Ipswich's Kelvin Davis keeping the score down.

The loss of David Vaughan due to a hamstring injury just prior to kick off gave Chris McCready the chance to get his first start of the season at left-back and Crewe dominated the first period with Steve Jones, Dean Ashton and Lunt all going close inside the first 20 minutes.

Davis made a string of impressive saves, including one outstanding stop from Ashton, but in the second half Ince was even more outstanding than his opposite number, with stunning stops from Darren Bent, Marcus Bent and Pablo Counago that earned him a deserved Man-of-the-Match award.

David Wright was another one of Crewe's many heroes when he headed Tommy Miller's effort off the line, but the game was ultimately settled in the 69th minute with a moment of magic from Lunt.

Some audacious skill from Ben Rix set up the opportunity as visiting centre back Drissa Diallo could only resort to a scything tackle to prevent the youngster's progress, and Lunt did the rest from 25 yards.

The Runcorn-born midfield man stepped up to take the free kick and sent a superb Beckham-esque curling shot into the top corner, which finally saw Davis beaten and the Alex on the road to their first league win of the season.

Dario's Comments
'We played very well, particularly in the first half. We scored a super goal though and it punished Ipswich because they gave away some silly fouls. The keeper invited him to put it there and Kenny put it in. I thought we stuck at it very well after that and although I was glad when the referee blew his final whistle we played very well.'

Joe Royle's Comments
'There is no way we deserved to lose. Crewe's 'keeper was man of the match and rightfully so, and how we have lost it I don't know. Crewe are a good club. They play a little bit more direct than they used to with Dean Ashton in the team, but they will be very difficult to beat at home. The goal was a great free kick but you could not blame our goalkeeper. He [Lunt] did what he did well.'

Sunday People
Dario Gradi's culture club celebrated their return to Division One with a champagne show in the sunshine. And if this performance is any guide, the prophets of doom who have predicted a speedy return to the Second Division for Crewe will soon be eating their words.

News of the World
Kenny Lunt took a leaf out of David Beckham's book by curling home a stunning free kick to steal the points for Crewe. The diminutive midfielder may not have Beckham's movie star looks but he has certainly got a touch of magic in his boots – as Ipswich found to their cost.

Dean Ashton is held back by Ipswich's Richard Naylor.

Kenny Lunt celebrates his winning free-kick against promotion candidates Ipswich Town.

Millwall 1

Whelan 90

Crewe Alexandra 1

Ashton 58

Millwall

1	Tony Warner
2	Matt Lawrence
3	Robbie Ryan
4	Tim Cahill
5	Stuart Nethercott
9	Neil Harris
11	Noel Whelan
12	Darren Ward
14	Andy Roberts
19	Dennis Wise
29	Bob Peeters

Substitutes

10	Richard Sadlier (Lawrence 77)
13	Willy Gueret
30	Charley Hearn (Ryan 77)
34	Paul Robinson
42	Juan (Peeters 62)

Referee

Mr S. Tomlin (Lewes)

Crewe Alexandra

1	Clayton Ince
2	David Wright
4	Kenny Lunt
5	Adie Moses
6	Stephen Foster
8	Dave Brammer
9	Steve Jones
10	Dean Ashton
11	David Vaughan
14	Ben Rix
19	Justin Cochrane

Substitutes

12	Lee Bell
13	Ademole Bankole
17	James Robinson
18	Chris McCready (Wright 82)
20	Allan Smart (Ashton 86)

MATCH REPORT

Crewe were cruelly denied all three points from their trip to the Den when Millwall's Noel Whelan popped up in stoppage time to head a late, late equaliser for Mark McGhee's side.

The Alex had taken a second-half lead after Dean Ashton capitalised on some comical defending from the home side, and the boys had looked comfortable until the dying seconds, when the Railwaymen capitulated with three points so nearly in the bag.

Dario welcomed David Vaughan back into the starting line up at left back and things were even in the first half with neither side particularly strong going forward. At the back Adie Moses was particularly effective, marshalling giant Millwall debutant Bob Peeters, while Steve Jones caused problems with his pace all afternoon.

Crewe took the lead after the break when Lions goalkeeper Tony Warner and defender Darren Ward conspired to get themselves in a real mess. Ashton flicked the ball on from a long clearance out of defence and began to chase it down as Ward shepherded it back towards his keeper. But neither Ward nor Warner took responsibility for clearing their line and after an embarrassing mix up Ashton guided the ball into an empty net to leave the away fans in rapturous applause.

The home side, now with the crowd on their backs, looked to respond, but neither Moses nor Stephen Foster were seriously troubled defensively, while Jones and Ashton caused continuous problems on the counter-attack.

But just when it looked as if the Alex would head back to South Cheshire with all three points, and with the scoreboard showing 13 seconds of normal time remaining, the Lions bit back.

Dario's Comments

'I didn't think we played all that well today, although we had the better of the chances throughout the game and with a bit of luck we could have held on. I thought our two centre-backs played well and coped well with their threat and Clayton Ince made two very good saves in the second half.'

Mark McGhee's Comments

'Dario would have been very upset if they [Crewe] had lost the game because they didn't deserve that. I thought Dennis [Wise] was going to score at the end but he said he stubbed his foot. It was a catastrophic error that gifted them their goal and so we did well to get a point.'

Sunday Sentinel

Dennis Wise missed a sitter in the final minute and that would have been awfully harsh on Dario Gradi's men. Alex boss Gradi said: 'It's disappointing to concede a late goal, but it was probably a fair result.'

The Times

Crewe's frustration at their failure to capitalise fully on their superior passing and chances was reflected in a succession of niggly offences that culminated in Dean Ashton being withdrawn by Dario Gradi, Crewe's proudly disciplinarian manager, before his yellow card was turned into red. Crewe the sinners? Millwall the saints?

Dave Brammer and Stephen Foster get to grips with Millwall substitute Richard Sadlier.

Tim Cahill finally got the better of Vaughan down the right flank and delivered a good quality cross into the box, and Whelan's glancing header flew into Clayton Ince's net via the upright.

Even then Crewe could have stolen the win, as substitute Allan Smart, making his Alex debut, drove down the left flank before delivering the ball into the box for Jones, who was just inches away from diverting it into the net. Dennis Wise missed an easy chance in the dying seconds that would have given the Lions an undeserved win, while Ashton was withdrawn by Dario late on to spare him a red card after being booked for making comments to a linesman.

Chris McCready deflects a Dennis Wise shot past the post.

Monday 25 August 2003 – 7.45pm – Gresty Road – Att: 7,026

Crewe Alexandra 1 Walsall 0

S. Jones 66

Crewe Alexandra

1	Clayton Ince
4	Kenny Lunt
5	Adie Moses
6	Stephen Foster
8	Dave Brammer
9	Steve Jones
10	Dean Ashton
11	David Vaughan
14	Ben Rix
18	Chris McCready
19	Justin Cochrane

Substitutes

3	Richard Walker
12	Lee Bell
13	Ademole Bankole
17	James Robinson
20	Allan Smart

Referee

Mr C. Cain (Bootle)

Walsall

1	James Walker
2	Darren Bazeley
3	Zigor Aranalde
4	Danny Hay
6	Ian Roper
7	Simon Osborn
9	Jorge Leitao
10	Paul Merson
12	Pedro Matias
18	Vinny Samways
26	Paul Ritchie

Substitutes

8	Steve Corica
11	Darren Wrack (Roper 74)
15	Neil Emblen (Osborn 88)
16	Gary Birch (Leitao 74)
50	Stefan Oakes

MATCH REPORT

The Railwaymen made it three wins out of three at Gresty Road when Steve Jones capitalised on a defensive error from former Crewe target Danny Hay to give the Alex all three points, in a performance Dario Gradi described as 'one of the best in my 20 years'.

Chris McCready returned to the starting line-up to replace the injured David Wright at full-back, but otherwise the Alex were unchanged as they looked to shrug off the disappointment of Millwall's last-minute equaliser two days earlier.

And the 7,000+ crowd were treated to a Bank Holiday Monday extravaganza as both sides played entertaining, free flowing, attacking football on a thoroughly enjoyable evening for the football purist.

The key though was the way Crewe dealt with the midfield wizardry of former England star Paul Merson, who tried in vain to conjure up a goal for the Saddlers but was expertly marshalled by the outstanding Dave Brammer, who easily claimed the Man-of-the-Match honours.

It was almost a shame that the winning goal came from such a poor defensive mistake on a night of such excellent football, but Crewe's home faithful were not complaining.

The crucial goal arrived in the 66th minute and it was the unfortunate Hay who gifted it to the home side. The big Kiwi inadvertently stood on the ball when trying to play it out of defence, allowing Jones to nip in and steal possession. The Northern Ireland international quickly spread the ball to Kenny Lunt in space, and although his fierce shot rattled the Walsall crossbar Jones was on hand to prod the ball home as Ian Roper dithered over his clearance on the goal-line.

Although some national papers credited the strike as a Roper own goal, Jones definitely got the final touch to his second goal of the season, but in truth no one associated with the Alex really cared. 1–0 to the Railwaymen.

Dario's Comments
'It was a terrific game of football by two excellent sides, who played the game in a skilful and clever way and who possess great ability. They played well but I thought we deservedly won the game because we created the better chances. We hit the post and had some other good opportunities and I thought we were magnificent and everybody played well.'

Colin Lee's Comments
'It was an entertaining game and both sides tried to play good football, but the winning goal proved to be an unfortunate defensive error. I always thought that it would take something like that to separate the two sides, because I thought we were evenly matched on the night.'

The Daily Star
Dopey Ian Roper handed Crewe three points by walking the ball into his own net last night. Walsall's big stopper found the ball at his feet in the 66th minute after Kenny Lunt's shot cannoned off the bar.

The Sun
Steve Jones grabbed his second goal of the season to end Walsall's unbeaten run. The Northern Ireland international won possession in midfield, played in Kenny Lunt and then pounced on the rebound when Lunt's shot hit the bar.

Dean Ashton bursts into the Walsall box during our 1-0 win over the Saddlers.

Burnley 1

Chaplow 52

Crewe Alexandra 0

Burnley

1	Brian Jensen
3	Mo Camara
5	David May
6	Graham Branch
7	Glen Little
8	Robbie Blake
10	Ian Moore
12	Tony Grant
15	Dean West
18	Luke Chadwick
20	Richard Chaplow

Substitutes

11	Alan Moore (Ian Moore 21)
17	Arthur Gnohere (Chaplow 87)
21	Matthew O'Neill
23	Paul Scott

Referee

Mr G. Laws (Whitley Bay)

Crewe Alexandra

1	Clayton Ince
2	David Wright
4	Kenny Lunt
5	Adie Moses
6	Stephen Foster
8	Dave Brammer
9	Steve Jones
10	Dean Ashton
11	David Vaughan
14	Ben Rix
19	Justin Cochrane

Substitutes

3	Richard Walker
7	Neil Sorvel (Cochrane 71)
13	Ademole Bankole
18	Chris McCready (Moses 70)
20	Allan Smart (Rix 77)

MATCH REPORT

Despite a decent performance and a Clayton Ince penalty save at Turf Moor, the Alex squandered a number of gilt-edged chances against the Clarets and ultimately paid the price as Richard Chaplow's first goal in senior football condemned the Railwaymen to a 1–0 defeat.

After welcoming David Wright back into the side, Dario's team was virtually at full strength for the clash with Stan Ternent's Lancashire outfit and the Alex started the game at a tremendous pace with Steve Jones once again causing all sorts of problems to the opposition rearguard.

He gave former Manchester United defender David May a difficult afternoon and could have covered himself in glory more than once in the first half. Jones had two efforts blocked and David Vaughan a shot saved inside 10 minutes, and when Burnley striker Ian Moore hobbled off injured, the game looked there for the taking.

But despite both sides playing some neat football, defences began to get on top, and it started to look as if the first goal of the game would be decisive.

And so it proved, as Burnley's match-winner arrived just seven minutes into the second period. Full-back Dean West created the goal with a forceful run and cross from the right, but young Chaplow, only in the side due to an injury to Paul Weller, took the richly deserved honours with a crisp shot into the bottom corner, which left Ince with no chance.

Glen Little's glaring miss raised the Crewe fans' spirits a few minutes later as the skilful Burnley winger blasted miles over the crossbar to the derision of the away end, but the home side should have sealed the game soon after. Dean Ashton was dubiously adjudged to have handballed in the area by a linesman 25 yards away, but Ince reacted superbly to push Robbie Blake's spot kick to safety and give the Alex hope.

But Ashton, Allan Smart and David Vaughan all missed chances to earn their side a point and Jones was desperately unlucky when his low shot struck the foot of the post. To make matters even worse the impressive Adie Moses limped off with a torn hamstring which would see him sidelined for several weeks.

All in all a disappointing afternoon's work.

Clayton Ince saved a Robbie Blake penalty at Turf Moor, but it still wasn't enough for the Alex.

September Review

Dario Gradi entered hospital for a heart valve replacement at the end of the month.

The month of September was a testing one for everyone connected with the football club. An outstanding comeback against Nottingham Forest was quickly overshadowed by the news that manager Dario Gradi had entered hospital in preparation for a pre-planned aortic heart valve replacement operation.

The country's longest-serving manager had known for a while that the operation would be needed at some stage, and when better to leave team affairs to his assistant Neil Baker and Academy Director Steve Holland than after our most outstanding performance of the season against Forest. 'Follow that' was the humorous way Dario decided to exit the dressing room after our stylish 3–1 home win.

Dario had undergone six months of testing at Leighton Hospital and at the Adidas HQ in Hazel Grove after the League Managers Association had discovered a minor problem in one of his heart valves. The condition sometimes left Dario out of breath and was in no way connected with the stresses of the game, as John Barnwell, the LMA's Chief Executive, pointed out at the time: 'I'm sure Dario would not blame his condition on the game, but it is always seen as an intense job in the public eye. Dario was one of 10 managers on our pilot scheme Fit For Football. He was one of the guinea pigs from day one. The findings and work on the programme is confidential to the manager and specialist, but this was a pre-planned operation and not an

Anthony Tonkin in action on his full league debut against West Ham.

stand after games. Examinations showed that my aortic valve in the heart would eventually need replacing. I felt that time was now.'

The boss added: 'In no way is this condition connected to stress and the surgeons have told me that I will have more energy now than before. I'm a bit battered and bruised and it will be a few more weeks before I've recovered fully.'

Remarkably, Dario would be back with us within a month and after gradually easing himself back into the role he carried on where he left off.

A busy month off the field also saw Jon Walters arrive on loan and then be recalled by Bolton Wanderers without him kicking a ball for the first team, and Allan Smart sign a season-long contract with us after previously impressing on a month-to-month agreement. The much-travelled striker didn't have much luck when it came to injuries, with a knee injury ending his season in the New Year.

On a more positive note, youngsters Dean Ashton and Ben Rix signed new and improved contracts to remain with us until 2006 and 2007 respectively. They joined the likes of Rich Walker, Steve Jones, Stephen Foster, David Vaughan and Neil Sorvel, who all agreed new deals at various times during the summer.

Anthony Tonkin finally signed from Stockport County for a fee rising to £175,000 depending on appearances, but as chairman John Bowler explained the Luke Rodgers deal became dead in the water due to Shrewsbury's over-inflated asking price: 'In essence the whole thing broke down because Shrewsbury were talking about £1 million, in other words as good as, if not better, than Rob Hulse. We didn't see it as anywhere near that.

'I think the truth of the matter is that Shrewsbury didn't want to let him go anyway, and I understand that because he may be pivotal in them getting back into the Football League at the first attempt. As soon as we realised that it wasn't just a negotiating stance then we decided to forget it and move on elsewhere.'

On the pitch, two wins and two defeats saw Crewe Alexandra in 12th position after nine matches.

emergency.' Other managers and coaches such as Neil Warnock of Sheffield United, John Rudge of Stoke City and Alex Ferguson of Manchester United all received various treatments throughout the season following check-ups with the LMA.

Obviously the news was a shock to a lot of people in and out of the game and the club was inundated with phone messages, get well cards, faxes, letters and emails. It was hugely appreciated by everyone at the Alex, and by none more so than Dario Gradi himself, who once his energy had returned answered every message personally. 'I would like to thank everyone for their concern and for all the cards and messages waiting for me at the football club,' said Dario after returning home. 'I'm sorry for the suddenness and the surprise but we felt that any advanced announcement would have caused a chaotic situation.'

He explained: 'About six years ago I realised that I was more out of breath than I should be when I was making my way up to the top of the

Rotherham United 0 Crewe Alexandra 2

Ashton 45 (penalty)
Walker 57

Rotherham United

1	Mike Pollitt
8	Chris Swailes
9	Martin Butler
12	Stewart Talbot
17	John Mullin
18	Scott Minto
20	Andy Monkhouse
22	Shaun Barker
23	Darren Byfield
24	Chris Sedgwick
28	Guy Branston

Substitutes

6	Julien Baudet (Talbot 80)
7	Mark Robins (Monkhouse 66)
11	Nick Daws
21	Bradley Jones
29	Richie Barker

Referee

Mr P. Robinson (East Yorkshire)

Crewe Alexandra

1	Clayton Ince
2	David Wright
3	Richard Walker
4	Kenny Lunt
6	Stephen Foster
8	Dave Brammer
9	Steve Jones
10	Dean Ashton
11	David Vaughan
14	Ben Rix
19	Justin Cochrane

Substitutes

7	Neil Sorvel (Vaughan 89)
13	Ademole Bankole
15	Luke Varney
16	Anthony Tonkin (Rix 73)
21	Paul Edwards (Jones 86)

MATCH REPORT

The Alex collected their first away win of the season in front of the Sky Television cameras, as central defender Richard Walker marked his return to the starting line up with a goal.

Walker, back in the team following an injury to Adie Moses, smuggled home a goal 12 minutes after the interval to put Crewe into cruise control, after the Railwaymen ended a scrappy first half display by taking the lead thanks to Dean Ashton's emphatic spot kick.

On a balmy afternoon in the South Yorkshire sunshine Crewe overcame the previous away defeat at Burnley by hardly getting out of first gear and still defeating a poor looking Rotherham side at Millmoor.

The first 20 minutes were almost totally devoid of goalmouth activity and the rest of the half wasn't much better, although Shaun Barker, Martin Butler and John Mullin all had half chances for the home side. Ashton also had a handful of opportunities for Crewe but in truth the over-fussiness of the referee completely spoiled this game.

All too often he disrupted the match with his constant whistle blowing, with Stephen Foster and Dave Brammer early entrants to his notebook, but in first-half stoppage time the Alex faithful had no complaints as the man in black awarded the Railwaymen a penalty.

In what must have been a rush of blood to the head, Rotherham's veteran defender Guy Branston decided to throttle Steve Jones by climbing all over him as Ashton's free kick whizzed into the area and the ref had no hesitation in awarding a spot kick. Ashton stepped up to blast home his third goal of the season and send the Alex into the dressing rooms for a half-time break in high spirits.

After the break, the Millers rarely threatened to get back in the game and it was effectively over as a contest after 57 minutes.

Dario's Comments
'When you come to Rotherham you expect a battle and a bit of a bombardment. We were panicking a little bit in the first half but they never really had a clear-cut chance. It was a penalty because their player held Jonah down and Dean thumped it. They are unstoppable and if the 'keeper puts his head there, it will take it off.'

Ronnie Moore's Comments
'We played like a pub team. We should be called the Rose and Crown, not Rotherham United. There are players out there who are not giving everything for this football club. They know who they are and they cannot be surprised when I leave them out of our next game with Sheffield United.'

Daily Telegraph
Dario Gradi, Britain's longest-serving manager, has never allowed himself to be carried away by the slings and arrows of football fortune. When it was put to him that his team had made a good start, Gradi just replied that if they had lost at Rotherham people would be saying they'd made a bad start!

The Times
Richard Walker showed why he is tipped to become a top football bouncer. The Crewe defender is built like a brick out house. And when you put that prison haircut on top of a 6ft 4in frame nobody is too surprised he is known by his teammates as 'the doorman'.

After winning a free kick on the right-hand edge of the box, Kenny Lunt swung in his usual perfect cross to the danger zone, and as Rotherham tried to clear Walker nipped in to scramble home from close range.

From then on the game fizzled out as a contest as Crewe cruised to victory with the only other noteworthy moment being Stephen Foster's perfectly timed last-ditch tackle on Darren Byfield, which topped another superb defensive display.

Richard Walker, Crewe Alexandra

Crewe Alexandra 0   West Ham United 3

Connolly 16, 21
Etherington 25

Crewe Alexandra

1	Clayton Ince
2	David Wright
3	Richard Walker
4	Kenny Lunt
6	Stephen Foster
8	Dave Brammer
9	Steve Jones
10	Dean Ashton
14	Ben Rix
16	Anthony Tonkin
19	Justin Cochrane

Substitutes

7	Neil Sorvel (Cochrane 77)
13	Ademole Bankole
15	Luke Varney
18	Chris McCready
21	Paul Edwards (Jones 73)

Referee

Mr A.N. Butler (Sutton-in-Ashfield)

West Ham

1	David James
2	Tomas Repka
5	Robert Lee
7	Christian Dailly
8	David Connolly
9	Jermain Defoe
12	Matthew Etherington
14	Wayne Quinn
16	Kevin Horlock
19	Ian Pearce
20	Niclas Alexandersson

Substitutes

15	Anton Ferdinand (Etherington 80)
22	Matthew Kilgallon (Quinn 27)
28	David Noble (Alexandersson 86)
32	Stephen Bywater
33	Neil Mellor

MATCH REPORT

Dario Gradi described his players as 'chokers' as first half defensive errors cost the Alex badly against promotion favourites West Ham United.

Crewe gifted the Hammers a 3–0 lead inside 25 minutes before really finding a foothold in the game, but by then any chance of taking anything from the fixture was well and truly over against Trevor Brooking's highly-rated young squad.

After being treated to a football feast against Walsall last time out at Gresty Road a near sell-out crowd was expecting more of the same against the Londoners, but the Railwaymen were rocked as David Connolly's quick-fire brace sent the Alex spinning to defeat.

With David Vaughan out, Dario Gradi handed a full debut to £175,000 signing Anthony Tonkin at left back, and although he was blameless in all three goals, teammates Stephen Foster and Clayton Ince both held their hands up to costly errors.

After just 16 minutes, Crewe were on the back foot when some sloppy defending by Foster allowed Connolly to pounce. Although immaculate in the games prior to this, Foster dithered in possession deep inside his own half before under-hitting a back pass towards Ince, which the former Wimbledon hitman gobbled up before sliding home a cool finish.

Five minutes later things went from bad to worse for the home side as Connolly received another gift of a goal to make it 2–0. This time Ince was the culprit as he spilled Wayne Quinn's 30-yard free kick and Connolly snapped up the opportunity from close range.

Crewe's players (and supporters) seemed visibly shell-shocked by this stage and when Matthew Etherington superbly half volleyed Quinn's corner into the back of the net on 24

Dario's Comments

'I said to the players before the game, "tonight we either play really well or we choke", and we choked. It's a question of what if tonight. I thought we started well and looked fine and I honestly thought it was going to be the game we all expected. The first goal was awful and the second was poor as well.'

Trevor Brooking's Comments

'I would have taken winning by the odd goal beforehand, so to win by three was very pleasing. After the first 15 minutes of the second half when Crewe really came at us, I thought we were comfortable.'

The Sentinel

Dario Gradi admitted his players choked under the pressure of playing promotion favourites West Ham. The Alex were well beaten 3–0 to the disappointment of the majority in a near sell-out Alexandra Stadium. Two woeful defensive mistakes by Steve Foster and 'keeper Clayton Ince helped the Hammers on their way as Crewe found themselves three down after just 25 minutes.

The Crewe Chronicle

Crewe crashed to their first home defeat of the season after gift-wrapping West Ham their first two goals at Gresty Road last night. The Alex found the going tough as Trevor Brooking stretched his unbeaten record as the Hammers' caretaker boss to 10 games in the first-ever league meeting between the two sides.

minutes to make it 3–0 a cricket score seemed a possibility.

To be fair to the players, after reaching the half-time interval with no further damage, they took the game to West Ham in the second period, but although David James was forced to make good saves from Dean Ashton and Kenny Lunt the game was lost in the madness of the opening 25 minutes.

West Ham defender Ian Pearce shadows Dean Ashton.

Ben Rix tried to inspire a Crewe revival in the second half.

Saturday 20 September 2003 – 3.00pm – Gresty Road– Att: 8,685

Crewe Alexandra 3 Nottingham Forest 1

Lunt 64
Ashton 74
S. Jones 88

Harewood 54

Crewe Alexandra

1	Clayton Ince
2	David Wright
3	Richard Walker
4	Kenny Lunt
6	Stephen Foster
8	Dave Brammer
9	Steve Jones
10	Dean Ashton
11	David Vaughan
14	Ben Rix
19	Justin Cochrane

Substitutes

7	Neil Sorvel
13	Ademole Bankole
16	Anthony Tonkin
18	Chris McCready
21	Paul Edwards

Referee

Mr M. Clattenburg (Northumberland)

Nottingham Forest

1	Darren Ward
2	Mathieu Louis-Jean
5	Michael Dawson
6	John Thompson
7	Andy Reid
8	Gareth Williams
10	Gareth Taylor
11	Marlon Harewood
21	Danny Sonner
22	Stephen McPhail
23	Wes Morgan

Substitutes

4	Des Walker
12	Barry Roche
14	Eoin Jess
17	Michael Stewart
18	Brynjar Gunnarsson

MATCH REPORT

Dario Gradi's final match before his scheduled heart valve replacement operation turned out to be a real cracker at Gresty Road.

After the error-ridden defeat against West Ham just four days earlier, Crewe's players really turned on the style in front of the home crowd against Nottingham Forest to secure a 3–1 win, in what Dario described as one of the best performances he had ever seen.

Although the players didn't know that their manager was heading into hospital the following day, they sent him off in superb style after coming from behind to totally outclass Forest and earn a richly deserved three points.

David Vaughan returned to the side in place of Anthony Tonkin at left back and both sides played some good football in the first half, although the game burst into life in the second period when Forest got an undeserved lead through Marlon Harewood.

The visitors danger man collected a neat pass from Andy Reid, on 52 minutes, before

David Vaughan accelerates away from Marlon Harewood.

Deano and Jonah celebrate our third goal against Forest.

lifting it over Clayton Ince and into the back of the net to stun the home crowd.

But, when in the past that goal would have signalled a Crewe collapse, it had exactly the opposite effect on the players now, who stepped up their game to reach new heights and fire themselves back into the game in style.

Kenny Lunt, on his 250th start for the club, brought the scoreline level with another masterful free kick.

Danny Sonner's clumsy challenge on Ben Rix handed Lunt the opportunity to repeat his heroics against Ipswich earlier in the season, and he duly obliged with a pin-point shot into the top corner of Darren Ward's goal.

Crewe were now rampant in attack, and David Wright struck the post after a blistering run forward, but 15 minutes from time the Railwaymen were deservedly in front thanks to Dean Ashton. The 19-year-old striker bagged his fourth goal of the season in the 74th minute when he met Dave Brammer's clipped cross with a well-placed header into the back of the net.

Instead of sitting back on the lead Crewe continued to pressurise Forest's failing defence and after going close on numerous occasions, Steve Jones wrapped up the points near the end. Ashton was desperately unfortunate to see his effort rattle the crossbar but Jones was alert enough to follow up and finish with a diving header.

Tuesday 23 September 2003 – 7.45pm – Walkers Stadium– Att: 27,675

Leicester City 1 Crewe Alexandra 0

Dickov (penalty) 82

Leicester City

1	Ian Walker
2	Andy Impey
3	Frank Sinclair
8	Lilian Nalis
10	James Scowcroft
12	Paul Brooker
21	Riccardo Scimeca
22	Paul Dickov
24	Steve Howey
27	Brian Deane
29	John Curtis

Substitutes

6	Muzzy Izzet (Scowcroft 45)
11	Jordan Stewart (Deane 38)
16	Danny Coyne
32	Billy McKinlay
34	Nicolas Priet (Brooker 89)

Referee

Mr A.R. Hall (Birmingham)

Crewe Alexandra

1	Clayton Ince
2	David Wright
3	Richard Walker
4	Kenny Lunt
6	Stephen Foster
8	Dave Brammer
10	Dean Ashton
11	David Vaughan
14	Ben Rix
19	Justin Cochrane
21	Paul Edwards

Substitutes

7	Neil Sorvel
13	Ademole Bankole
15	Luke Varney (Cochrane 89)
16	Anthony Tonkin (Rix 59)
18	Chris McCready

MATCH REPORT

Caretaker boss Neil Baker was cruelly denied an impressive result on his managerial debut by a controversial late penalty decision against Leicester at the Walkers Stadium.

After producing a performance full of guts and determination against the Premiership new boys it was a horrible way to go out of the Carling Cup after referee Mr Hall spotted a foul by David Wright on Jordan Stewart and Paul Dickov duly despatched the resulting spot kick with just eight minutes remaining.

Although Baker was desperately disappointed with the final scoreline he had every reason to be proud of his players' performance on the night, as they matched the Foxes in every department all evening.

Crewe's best chance fell to youngster Paul Edwards, making his full debut in place of the injured Steve Jones, but he was denied a dream start by some spectacular defending. Dean Ashton challenged England goalkeeper Ian Walker for a high cross in the area, and when the ball dropped, Edwards seemed certain to score from close range, but somehow Steve Howey got back to block his goal-bound shot on the line.

Earlier Walker had made several good saves from Ashton and Rix, while his best was a splendid tip over to deny Justin Cochrane his first goal for the club. At the other end Clayton Ince made two equally good saves from Lilian Nalis, who seemed to shoot on sight from wherever he received possession.

Ince also denied Dickov in the 74th minute with a spectacular tip over, but it was the former Manchester City forward who had the last laugh when he stroked home the controversial penalty just when it seemed the tie was destined for extra time.

Neil Baker's Comments

'That was a good performance from our players. They worked hard and defended superbly well. We knew that we would have to defend well and frustrate them and I thought we did that. The penalty decision looks harsh and I will have to wait to see what it looks like on the video because it is either a mistake by David Wright or by the referee.'

Micky Adams's Comments

'I'm glad to be in the hat for the next round but it was not a good performance from us this evening. I thought the Crewe boys were a credit to Dario and I wish him all the best for a speedy recovery.'

The Sun

Paul Dickov's penalty saved Leicester's blushes as Crewe put up a dogged display for sick boss Dario Gradi. Ref Andy Hall awarded the spot-kick for David Wright's 82nd minute foul on Jordan Stewart and Dickov made no mistake.

The Daily Telegraph

Dario Gradi's recovery from a heart operation will undoubtedly have quickened if he had been listening to last night's encounter with Leicester on hospital radio. Gradi's Crewe came within inches of securing a notable Premiership scalp after controlling most of the match but were denied victory by Paul Dickov's 80th minute penalty.

Cardiff City 3   Crewe Alexandra 0

Thorne 44, 85
Earnshaw 52

Cardiff City

1	Neil Alexander
2	Rhys Weston
3	Chris Barker
6	Daniel Gabbidon
8	Graham Kavanagh
10	Robert Earnshaw
11	Peter Thorne
12	Willie Boland
15	Mark Bonner
21	Tony Vidmar
25	Richard Langley

Substitutes

5	Spencer Prior
9	Andy Campbell (Earnshaw 84)
13	Martyn Margetson
16	Gary Croft (Boland 87)
17	James Collins (Thorne 89)

Referee
Mr A. Wiley (Burntwood)

Crewe Alexandra

1	Clayton Ince
2	David Wright
3	Richard Walker
4	Kenny Lunt
6	Stephen Foster
8	Dave Brammer
10	Dean Ashton
11	David Vaughan
16	Anthony Tonkin
19	Justin Cochrane
21	Paul Edwards

Substitutes

7	Neil Sorvel
12	Lee Bell
13	Ademole Bankole
15	Luke Varney (Edwards 81)
18	Chris McCready (Wright 45)

MATCH REPORT

Defensive errors reared their ugly heads once more as a bad mistake gifted Cardiff a goal just before half time and undid all Crewe's good work of the first period by signalling a second-half collapse at Ninian Park.

Caretaker manager Neil Baker's first league match in charge of the team had been going well for 44 minutes against the Bluebirds, and the back four had nullified the threat of the league's top scorer Robert Earnshaw, but Richard Walker's missed clearance at the end of the first period gift-wrapped Peter Thorne a goal and the seeds of Crewe's downfall were sown.

After weathering an early storm, the Alex had grabbed a foothold in the game midway through the first half, with Dean Ashton testing the reactions of Cardiff 'keeper Neil Alexander, but just before the break the capitulation began.

Graham Kavanagh put the Crewe defence under pressure with a forceful run into the box and when Walker failed to clear his cross Peter Thorne was on hand to fire in from close range.

It was a disastrous way to end the half and things got worse after the break when Earnshaw finally broke his shackles and doubled Cardiff's lead. This time Stephen Foster came in for criticism as he let the Welsh international off his leash for a second, which was all the time he needed to latch onto Kavanagh's pass and slide a shot beyond the reaches of Clayton Ince.

Walker, full debutant Paul Edwards and Dean Ashton all went close to halving the deficit over the next 20 minutes, but the game was over four minutes from time when the impressive Thorne, who only played after making a miracle recovery from a neck injury, scored his second and Cardiff's third of the game.

The former Stoke City man collected Chris Barker's cross on his chest before firing past Ince to end a thoroughly miserable afternoon for the Railwaymen.

Neil Baker's Comments
'Any defeat hurts and this does because we had been fairly comfortable going into the break. It hurts everyone and we didn't defend well enough today. If you make mistakes like we did then we haven't got much chance.'

Lennie Lawrence's Comments
'Anything other than a win would have been a travesty. I decided to give my defence another chance and they came up trumps with a clean sheet.'

The Sun
Crewe boss Dario Gradi who is in hospital after heart surgery received a lousy get well present. Peter Thorne helped Cardiff end a run of three straight defeats with goals in the 44th and 85th minutes while Robert Earnshaw pitched in with his 14th of the season.

News of the World
Dario Gradi will not be feeling any more cheerful today after the depressing news from South Wales. The Crewe manager is in hospital after undergoing heart surgery this week. And his deputy Neil Baker admitted: 'This won't do his recovery any good at all.'

David Wright injures his shoulder by denying Richard Langley a certain goal.

Dean Ashton does his defensive duty at a corner against the Bluebirds.

October Review

After missing just five matches, Dario Gradi returned to the hustle and bustle of football management in mid-October. He made an emotional return to action to oversee the 3–0 win over Derby County at the Alexandra Stadium.

In his absence the team had struggled to build on their encouraging start to the season and the loss of captain Dave Brammer through injury hardly helped matters. Neil Baker and Steve Holland worked exceptionally hard in their temporary roles but didn't really have much luck on their side. Their league record of three defeats, one draw and finally that elusive win over George Burley's Derby County was not a true reflection of the performances. We hit the woodwork three times against Coventry before eventually going down 2–0 at Highfield Road and then let a two-goal lead slip at home to struggling Bradford City. Leicester City also ended our hopes of an extended run in the Carling Cup with Paul Dickov converting an extremely dubious late penalty at the Walkers Stadium.

In a difficult month, Crewe Alexandra also failed to break down a stubborn Watford defence after they had been reduced to 10 men early on after their goalkeeper Alec Chamberlain had

Dario Gradi returned to Gresty Road after undergoing a heart valve replacement. He was away for just four weeks.

Justin Cochrane had an outstanding debut season with us after signing from Hayes.

handled outside his penalty area. You could sense the archetype smash and grab scenario occurring well before Danny Webber's smart finish on the hour mark. Dario, who couldn't bear to listen to the games on the radio, wasn't too pleased when he watched a re-run of those games on his trusted video recorder!

'The last few games have been frustrating because I think that the players have thrown them away,' said a disappointed Dario. 'That has nothing to do with Neil (Baker), Steve (Holland) or me, it is down to them. They know what to do and they didn't do it and there is nothing my coming back will do about it. It's up to them.

'The players shouldn't have missed me at all. I won't be saying anything that they haven't heard before.

'I wasn't too interested after the operation. When you're lying in a hospital bed feeling groggy you don't really care what's happening at

Crewe Alexandra. But Neil came to see me after the Coventry game with the video and from that moment on I've been actively involved.'

A hectic month on and off the field ended with our derby clash with Stoke City, the first in five years, and we should have won it too, considering the number of chances we created at a highly charged Britannia Stadium.

Steve Jones's 54th-minute opener on his 27th birthday appeared to be enough to claim all three points until Stoke substitute Chris Greenacre capitalised on some poor defending to grab a late leveller.

Even then on-loan striker Andrew Barrowman had a chance to win it for us in stoppage time, but he tamely shot into the legs of Dutchman Ed de Goey and we had to make do with a share of the spoils. It proved to be Barrowman's last touch in Crewe colours because Dario soon returned him to St Andrews.

The return of Dario evidently revitalised results with the month ending on a high with home wins over Derby and Preston North End and that draw at Stoke City.

Away from the pitch youngsters Carl Frost (Witton Albion) and Lee Bell (Shrewsbury Town) were allowed to gain some first-team experience after falling down the pecking order at Gresty Road.

In search of some more firepower up front, Neil Baker succeeded in bringing in Barrowman on a month's loan and his arrival had the desired effect with both Steve Jones and Dean Ashton responding positively to the increased competition.

Trying to bring in Barrowman's Birmingham teammate, the American Jovan Kirovski, proved to be a more complicated business because of work permit requirements and Baker decided against pursuing the deal.

Ashton's continued form saw him called up for David Platt's Under-21 side that travelled to Istanbul for the last of their European Championship qualifiers and Steve Jones became a regular member of Sammy McIlroy's Northern Ireland squad. David Vaughan also received international recognition, even scoring his first international goal in an 8–1 defeat by an impressive Italian Under-21 side in Pavia.

Wednesday 1 October 2003 – 7.45pm – Highfield Road – Attendance 11,557

Coventry City 2 Crewe Alexandra 0

McAllister 49
Morrell 73

Coventry City

1	Scott Shearer
2	Andrew Whing
4	Mo Konjic
5	Richard Shaw
6	Youssef Safri
9	Dele Adebola
10	Gary McAllister
11	Graham Barrett
12	Andy Morrell
15	Claus Jorgensen
18	Steve Staunton

Substitutes

20	Calum Davenport
21	Julian Joachim (Adebola 45)
26	Stephen Warnock (Safri 85)
35	Yazid Mansouri (Jorgensen 70)
36	Peggy Arphexad

Referee

Mr J. Ross (Essex)

Crewe Alexandra

1	Clayton Ince
2	David Wright
3	Richard Walker
4	Kenny Lunt
6	Stephen Foster
7	Neil Sorvel
9	Steve Jones
10	Dean Ashton
11	David Vaughan
14	Ben Rix
19	Justin Cochrane

Substitutes

12	Lee Bell (Rix 60)
13	Ademole Bankole
16	Anthony Tonkin
18	Chris McCready
19	Paul Edwards (Lunt 81)

MATCH REPORT

The record books will state that Crewe Alexandra suffered their third successive away defeat at the hands of Coventry City, but the 2–0 scoreline could have been awfully different if we had enjoyed the rub of the green on the night.

David Vaughan shields possession from Graham Barrett.

Dean Ashton had a first-minute goal ruled out for offside before Kenny Lunt twice hit the post from free-kicks in the first half, and Steve

Neil Baker's Comments

'There is a very thin line between winning and losing and that is what I've told the players in the dressing room. I thought we were unlucky at times but that is what happens. There isn't always that much in it.'

Gary McAllister's Comments

'We rode our luck at times this evening but I thought we just about shaded it when it came to the chances. I was pleased to score the first goal and Andy Morrell took his goal very well. I couldn't really see Crewe coming back into it after that but Scott (Shearer) made some fine saves at crucial times to keep us in at times.'

Daily Mail

Hopefully, a recovering Dario Gradi did not listen to this game on the radio after his team hit the woodwork on three occasions before going down 2–0 to a Coventry City side, who were desperate for some points of their own after an indifferent start.

Daily Mirror

A luckless Crewe saw a combination of Kenny Lunt's well-struck free kicks and Steve Jones hit the woodwork three times at Highfield Road. A piece of inspirational management from Gary McAllister at half time saw Joachim breathe new life into the Coventry attack – but it was in a playing capacity that the former Scottish international made his mark with his first goal of the season.

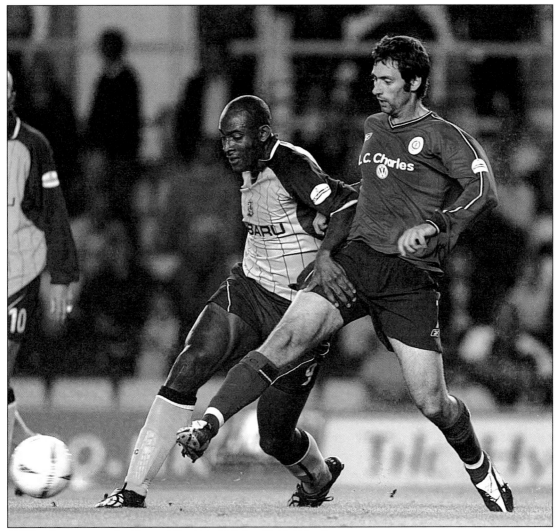

Neil Sorvel comes up against Crewe old boy Dele Adebola at Highfield Road.

Jones did the same once in the second after racing clear of Richard Shaw.

Neil Sorvel returned to the starting line-up for the first time with Dave Brammer ruled out with a groin strain. The captain's armband was passed on to Kenny Lunt.

In an entertaining game both sides had a number of opportunities to take the lead in the first half. Clayton Ince denied Andrew Whing, Youssef Safri and former Crewe players Graham Barrett and Dele Adebola. Ben Rix was also in the right place at the right time to prevent a Mo Konjic header from crossing the line.

At the other end, Sorvel returned a half-volley with interest when a David Vaughan corner broke to him. Ashton also blazed over from a good position after fine approach play from Jones before Lunt struck the post for the second time on the stroke of half time.

Lively substitute Julian Joachim replaced the ineffective Adebola at the interval and it wasn't long before the former Aston Villa forward was causing mayhem. It was his cross that was headed home by player-manager Gary McAllister in the 49th minute and he forced the free-kick from Rich Walker that led the killer second goal on 73 minutes. Safri's dangerous free-kick allowed Andy Morrell to glance a header past a helpless Ince to leave the Alex with an uphill struggle.

Crewe continued to press forward looking for a breakthrough and both centre-halves Walker and Foster went close to setting up a grandstand finish only to be denied by Scott Shearer in the Coventry goal.

Crewe Alexandra 0 Watford 1

Webber 61

Crewe Alexandra

1   Clayton Ince
2   David Wright
3   Richard Walker
4   Kenny Lunt
6   Stephen Foster
7   Neil Sorvel
9   Steve Jones
10 Dean Ashton
11 David Vaughan
18 Chris McCready
19 Justin Cochrane

Substitutes

13 Ademole Bankole
14 Ben Rix (Cochrane 45)
15 Luke Varney
16 Anthony Tonkin
19 Paul Edwards (McCready 45)

Referee

Mr F. Stretton (Nottinghamshire)

Watford

1   Alec Chamberlain
2   Neil Ardley
3   Paul Robinson
4   Paolo Vernazza
5   Neil Cox
7   Bruce Dyer
9   Danny Webber
12 Gavin Mahon
15 Marcus Gayle
21 Scott Fitzgerald
32 Stephen Kelly

Substitutes

6   Sean Dyche
17 Jamie Hand (Mahon 45)
19 Jerel Ifil (Webber 78)
22 Lee Cook
30 Lenny Pidgeley (Dyer 20)

MATCH REPORT

Ten-man Watford inflicted only Crewe's second home defeat of the season. Former Manchester United trainee Danny Webber scored the only goal of the game just after the hour mark to condemn the Alex to their fourth successive defeat.

Neil Sorvel enjoys a midfield tussle with Scott Fitzgerald.

Everything was on course for another home victory when goalkeeper Alec Chamberlain was sent off for handling outside the penalty area in the 20th minute, but the reduction in numbers seemed to inspire Ray Lewington's side. Substitute 'keeper Lenny Pidgeley replaced the unfortunate Bruce Dyer and was a constant thorn in our side. The on-loan

Neil Baker's Comments
'It was woeful today. It was absolutely woeful. We didn't play well before the sending-off and then they defended deep and we didn't have the ability in the team to break them down. We will be doing some more work out on the training ground that's for sure.'

Ray Lewington's Comments
'If you can get ahead when everything is going against you then it can inspire the players and that is what happened today. We got ahead and sometimes all the composure that teams like Crewe have goes out of the window. People thought we didn't have any spirit at this club but now we have proved them wrong.'

News of the World
Danny Webber's clinical finish fired 10-man Watford to victory at Crewe as Ray Lewington's men showed they have the stomach for a relegation fight. The Hornets went into the game without an away win all season but Danny Webber's strike changed that.

The Times
Watford survived the first-half dismissal of Alec Chamberlain to claim an unlikely victory. The goalkeeper was sent off after 19 minutes for handling outside of the area, and Lenny Pidgeley, on loan from Chelsea, responded brilliantly to his call.

Rich Walker gets a grip on Watford's match winner Danny Webber.

Chelsea youngster was well positioned to prevent Stephen Foster and Dean Ashton before Rich Walker had a goal chalked off for a foul on the 'keeper following a Kenny Lunt free kick.

Crewe looked the more likely to go on and win the game but with the experienced Marcus Gayle and Neil Cox at the back we found it difficult to break down their resilient defence.

The unexpected sucker-punch arrived in the 61st minute, when midfielder Jamie Hand capitalised on a David Vaughan stumble and released lone striker Webber. He kept his cool to slot home the only goal

of a frustrating game. With the goal advantage, Watford protected their lead as if their lives depended on it and with Crewe notably out-of-sorts we huffed and puffed but failed to break the door down.

The home supporters made their feelings known at the final whistle, but without Dario and our fair share of luck it was a time for sticking together and coming through our first real bad patch of the season.

To make matters even worse, Chris McCready and Justin Cochrane didn't reappear for the second half and joined our expanding injury list.

Crewe Alexandra 2 Bradford City 2

S. Jones 46
Ashton 49

Evans 55
Muirhead 87

Crewe Alexandra

1	Clayton Ince
2	David Wright
3	Richard Walker
4	Kenny Lunt
6	Stephen Foster
7	Neil Sorvel
9	Steve Jones
10	Dean Ashton
11	David Vaughan
14	Ben Rix
19	Justin Cochrane

Substitutes

13	Ademole Bankole
17	James Robinson
21	Paul Edwards
27	Adam Yates
28	Andrew Barrowman (Rix 89)

Referee

Mr M. Ryan (Lancashire)

Bradford City

29	Marlon Beresford
4	Thomas Kearney
5	David Wetherall
7	Paul Evans
9	Nicky Summerbee
11	Andy Gray
17	Jason Gavin
18	Ben Muirhead
19	Gareth Edds
21	Danny Forrest
22	Wayne Jacobs

Substitutes

13	Mark Paston
15	Simon Francis (Kearney 74)
20	Robert Wolleaston
23	Frazer McHugh
25	Michael Standing

MATCH REPORT

Crewe Alexandra's caretaker manager Neil Baker achieved the response he wanted from his players following the 1–0 home defeat to Watford – but it was still not enough to secure all three points against a struggling Bradford side.

The loan signing of Birmingham City forward Andrew Barrowman certainly fired Crewe's front two into life with both Steve Jones and Dean Ashton on target within the first five minutes of the second period.

Jones calmly rounded Marlon Beresford to score his fourth goal of the campaign after being released by Ben Rix before Dean Ashton, who had earlier struck a post, doubled our advantage three minutes later with a headed goal from a David Wright cross. It was Deano's fifth goal of the campaign and one that proved that the unfair criticism placed at his feet after the Watford game had not troubled him.

2–0 ahead and cruising, the Alex defence switched off at a corner and Paul Evans acrobatically got Bradford back into the game. Without a win in the last four matches anxiety began to set in as Nicky Law's side went in search of an equaliser.

The goal seemed to breathe some life into the visitors and with such an inexperienced bench Neil Baker didn't have too many options when it came to relieving the pressure in the closing stages.

Luck seemed to be on our side for once when Andy Gray missed an absolute sitter from underneath the crossbar on 76 minutes and then a stretching Rich Walker got just enough contact on a Danny Forrest shot to deflect it wide of the post.

Just when it appeared Crewe were going to hold on to the points, the impressive Ben Muirhead struck a beauty to snatch a point with two minutes remaining. It was rather cruel for us because we had been the better side for most of the match, but credit must also go to the Bantams who were on a dreadful run themselves, with six games without a win.

Neil Baker's Comments
'We've arrested the slide and haven't lost which is good, although our defending was poor for their two goals. It was a strange game though. We started a lot better than we did against Watford and played some good football. The lads worked hard and tried to play although we were finding it hard to get Kenny and Ben into the game.'

Nicky Law's Comments
'We gave away two poor goals but you have to commend the positives. We gave ourselves a mountain to climb but scored another two wonder goals and I thought we could have gone on to win it. The players didn't let their heads go down, they stuck together and played some good stuff.'

The Sun
Bradford deservedly snatched an unlikely point with time running out. Paul Evans's wonder strike gave them a lifeline and they seemed to grow in confidence the longer the game went on. Crewe looked comfortable until that point and temporary manager Neil Baker will be disappointed to see a two-goal lead slip away.

The Daily Express
Crewe Alexandra saw three home points slip away after scoring twice in three second-half minutes. Ben Muirhead's late leveller gave a spirited Bradford side a share of the spoils in an entertaining second half.

Rich Walker keeps tabs on Bradford full-back Wayne Jacobs.

Steve Jones battles for possession with Jason Gavin.

Crewe Alexandra 3 Derby County 0

Barrowman 10
Ashton 24
Rix 78

Crewe Alexandra

1	Clayton Ince
2	David Wright
3	Richard Walker
4	Kenny Lunt
6	Stephen Foster
8	Dave Brammer
9	Steve Jones
10	Dean Ashton
11	David Vaughan
19	Justin Cochrane
28	Andrew Barrowman

Substitutes

7	Neil Sorvel (Brammer 44)
13	Ademole Bankole
14	Ben Rix (Barrowman 74)
20	Allan Smart
29	Billy Jones (Cochrane 86)

Referee
Mr M. Warren (Walsall)

Derby County

1	Lee Grant
2	Luciano Zavagno
6	Pablo Mills
7	Ian Taylor
9	Daniele Dichio
10	Michael Johnson
11	Lee Morris
12	Simo Valakari
14	Richard Jackson
29	Tom Huddlestone
30	Lee Holmes

Substitutes

5	Steve Elliott (Zavagno 84)
8	Candido Costa (Morris 66)
15	Adam Bolder
23	Marcus Tudgay (Valakari 74)
24	Lee Camp

MATCH REPORT

The return of manager Dario Gradi and captain Dave Brammer coincided with Crewe's first win in six matches. The reappearance of Dario just 27 days after his heart operation gave the players and home crowd a much-needed lift for the visit of Derby County.

Dario returned to the touchline against his former club Derby County.

Neil Baker and Steve Holland still had the responsibility of selecting the team for this one after working with and preparing the players all week. That meant a full debut for on-loan forward Andrew Barrowman and a recall for the fit-again Dave Brammer, who had missed the last three games due to groin strain. Unfortunately, his comeback lasted no more

Dario Gradi's Comments
'It's nice to be back. I think the game was very similar to the one during the week really. We got the goals, had a bit of a wobble, but didn't concede, which is the big difference to Tuesday, although we rode our luck a little bit at times. I haven't got any magic words. There's nothing that me, Neil or Steve can do. It's down to the players.'

George Burley's Comments
'From our point of view it was a strange game because we had most of the play and had a few chances of our own but we ended up losing 3-0. Ian's tackle led to the first yellow card and then he got the second for pulling the lad up.

The Daily Mail
Crewe's first victory in six games was just what the doctor ordered for Dario Gradi who was back at Gresty Road to see his side defeat Derby County 3-0.

The Daily Star
Loan signing Andrew Barrowman set Crewe on their way to victory with the opening goal on 10 minutes. The Birmingham youngster struck from close range to guide home a pass from Dean Ashton after he had missed a one-on-one situation with the Derby goalkeeper.

than 44 minutes as he suffered a reoccurrence of the injury that in time would mean surgery.

Crewe romped into a 10th-minute lead with Barrowman finishing off a flowing move at the second attempt. The predatory instincts of the young Scot saw him have the easy task of tapping home Dean Ashton's pass after Lee Grant had saved Barrowman's original effort.

A vibrant Crewe doubled the lead on 24 minutes after Barrowman repaid Ashton for his unselfishness by playing a part in a fine team goal. Barrowman latched on to a through ball from Brammer to feed Steve Jones, who crossed from the left wing. A rejuvenated Ashton made no mistake with a superbly taken volley.

In reply, Derby offered very little in terms of attacking play with Rich Walker earning the sponsors' Man-of-the-Match award for his performance up against the towering Daniele Dichio.

Substitute Ben Rix rounded off a memorable day with the first league goal of his career after the Derby defence got themselves in a right muddle. To make matters worse for the visitors, captain Ian Taylor flipped in injury time and was sent off for an awful foul on David Wright and then unsporting behaviour.

The game also saw Billy Jones make his debut for the club at the age of 16. The England Under-16 captain was given a taste of the action with five minutes of the game remaining. Ironically, the player who had recommended Billy to the club, Dave Walton, was there to witness it as a travelling member of the Derby contingent.

Dave Brammer unfortunately suffered a re-occurrence of his pelvic injury against the Rams.

Tuesday 21 October 2003 – 7.45pm – Gresty Road – Att: 7,012

Crewe Alexandra 2 Preston North End 1

Lunt 10
Foster 28

Etuhu 90

Crewe Alexandra

1	Clayton Ince
2	David Wright
3	Richard Walker
4	Kenny Lunt
6	Stephen Foster
7	Neil Sorvel
9	Steve Jones
10	Dean Ashton
11	David Vaughan
19	Justin Cochrane
28	Andrew Barrowman

Substitutes

13	Ademole Bankole
14	Ben Rix (Barrowman 71)
16	Anthony Tonkin
20	Allan Smart (Ashton 86)
29	Billy Jones

Referee

Mr H. Webb (Rotherham)

Preston North End

40	Jonathan Gould
2	Graham Alexander
3	Brian O'Neil
5	Michael Jackson
6	Marlon Broomes
9	Ricardo Fuller
16	Paul McKenna
17	Eddie Lewis
20	Chris Lucketti
25	Richard Cresswell

Substitutes

4	Dickson Etuhu
7	Lee Cartwright (O'Neil 65)
11	David Healy
13	Andrew Lonergan
15	Rob Edwards

MATCH REPORT

First-half goals from Kenny Lunt and Stephen Foster proved enough to see Crewe record their second home win in three days over promotion hopefuls Preston North End. For the second game running, the Alex raced into a two-goal lead with Lunt scoring his first goal in open play after 10 minutes and Foster heading his first goal of the season from a David Vaughan corner.

In between our two goals, Preston full-back Graham Alexander struck a post with a dipping volley and captain Chris Lucketti should have done better with a header from an Eddie Lewis corner.

Despite those scares, Crewe were full of confidence and played some fluent one-touch football. Vaughan forced Scottish international Jonathan Gould into an early save from a free kick and both Dean Ashton and Andrew Barrowman came close to extending our lead before the break.

Jamaican international Ricardo Fuller pressed the self-destruct button on 34 minutes, striking out with his elbow at his marker Richard Walker in front of a vigilant linesman. Fuller was shown the red card but refused to leave the field for the best part of five minutes. A member of the Preston backroom staff eventually ushered off the highly rated striker, but Crewe had a numerical advantage for the third time in four games .

It was vital that we didn't concede early in the second half and the defence restricted the visitors to shots from distance. Paul McKenna, Michael Keane and Richard Cresswell all had efforts saved by Clayton Ince.

At the important end, Dean Ashton struck the side netting after being found by the outstanding Vaughan and Steve Jones repeated the act after stealing a yard on former Crewe defender Michael Jackson.

Neil Sorvel retains the ball under pressure from American Eddie Lewis

Substitute Dickson Etuhu ended our hopes of a second consecutive clean sheet with a bizarre cross-cum-shot in injury time, but it was too little too late and Crewe deservedly held on to gain all three points. It was a result that put us healthily into 11th place in the league table. Next up were near neighbours Stoke City.

Steve Jones gave Scottish full-back Graham Alexander a tough night at Gresty Road

Stoke City 1

Greenacre 90

Crewe Alexandra 1

S. Jones 54

Stoke City

1	Ed de Goey
3	Clive Clarke
6	Clint Hill
7	Carl Asaba
9	Gifton Noel-Williams
10	Ade Akinbiyi
17	Darel Russell
20	Keith Andrews
21	John Halls
23	Karl Henry
29	Paul Williams

Substitutes

8	Chris Greenacre (Akinbiyi 74)
12	Neil Cutler
18	Lewis Neal (Henry 78)
24	Kris Commons (Clarke 29)
25	Gareth Owen

Referee

Mr R. Beeby (Northampton)

Crewe Alex

1	Clayton Ince
2	David Wright
3	Richard Walker
4	Kenny Lunt
6	Stephen Foster
7	Neil Sorvel
9	Steve Jones
10	Dean Ashton
11	David Vaughan
19	Justin Cochrane
28	Andrew Barrowman

Substitutes

13	Ademole Bankole
14	Ben Rix
16	Anthony Tonkin (Jones 75)
20	Allan Smart
29	Billy Jones

MATCH REPORT

The seventh meeting between ourselves and neighbours Stoke City ended in a 1–1 draw at the Britannia Stadium but it was certainly two points lost from our point of view! Steve Jones's fifth goal of the season on his 27th birthday looked to be enough to win this derby encounter, only for substitute Chris Greenacre to convert a late chance and save the home side's blushes.

Even then Andrew Barrowman had a chance to secure the local bragging rights in stoppage time but his shot hit the legs of Ed de Goey after he had been sent clear by Neil Sorvel. It proved to be the last action of the derby and Barrowman's last touch for the Alex. He was later left out against Reading and Sheffield United before returning to Birmingham soon afterwards.

Barrowman wasn't the only player to miss a chance in a second period that Crewe virtually dominated. De Goey was certainly the busier of the two goalkeepers and the Dutchman was called upon to deny both Dean Ashton and Justin Cochrane as we pressurized the Stoke goal.

Jonah's opener came after de Goey failed to hold a fierce drive from Ashton and our Northern Ireland international reacted first to convert the rebound. From there we should have gone on and won the game, but as you well know you have to score when you're on top.

Saying that, we were denied a blatant penalty when Gifton Noel-Williams manhandled Richard Walker in the penalty area and the referee was the only person in the stadium who missed the infringement.

Stoke substitute Kris Commons certainly made a difference to the Stoke side and he had a couple of efforts from long range before Greenacre's heartbreaking equaliser. The Crewe defence failed to clear a routine corner and Greenacre popped up in the right place at just the right time for the Potters to turn in Carl Asaba's lofted pass.

Birthday boy Steve Jones celebrates his opener against Stoke City.

November Review

Billy Jones became the latest Academy graduate to catch the eye in the Crewe first team after Dario rewarded his rapid progress with his full debut against Sunderland. Having been recommended to the club by former defender David Walton, the Shrewsbury-born talent proved to be the find of the season. His versatile performances at full-back, centre-half and in the centre of midfield captured the essence of what the club stands for.

Clayton Ince kept another two clean sheets at Gresty Road in November.

Despite being just 16 years of age at the time of his debut, Billy possesses the strength, technique, ability and temperament to cope with the rigours of First Division football and at Crewe he was given his chance to progress quickly.

The month began on a high with yet another home victory over one of the potential promotion candidates. A single goal from Steve Jones took his own personal tally to six and at the same time put a huge dent in Reading's aspirations for another end of season play-off appearance.

Sunderland were also beaten rather convincingly at what was fast becoming known as 'fortress Gresty Road', with twin strikers Steve Jones with a brace and Dean Ashton inflicting the damage on Mick McCarthy's shell-shocked side.

While our home form continued to have the rest of the First Division sitting up and taking note, our away record prevented us from making a serious push for those top six places. A miserable 2–0 away defeat at Gillingham was only worsened by Kenny Lunt's first red card of his career. The normally placid midfielder received his second yellow card of the afternoon following an ugly skirmish with the home side's player-manager Andy Hessenthaler on the touchline. It typified the frustration of the day.

Further away defeats followed at Sheffield United and newly installed title favourites Norwich City, who could call on loan starlets Peter Crouch and Darren Huckerby to unlock the Crewe defence. Rather alarmingly, we had now scored just once in our last seven away fixtures.

November also saw our stranglehold on the Cheshire Senior Cup come to an abrupt end at Witton Albion. Having established a 3–1 lead, the 'reserves' should have gone on to win the game quite comfortably, only for defensive mistakes to see the non-leaguers force extra-time and then remarkably complete the comeback. Mike Moseley was the Witton hero on the night, scoring the winner from the penalty spot after the referee had awarded a retake for encroachment.

Witnessing our surrender of the trophy we had proudly held for the previous two years was Dario Gradi, who, putting it mildly, was far from impressed by the performances of those players trying to stake a claim to a place in his first team: 'The Cheshire Senior Cup gives us an opportunity to look for those players we think can go on and play in the first team and we were left very disappointed with what we saw at Witton,' said the boss. 'We cannot continue waiting for people to fulfil their potential because they cannot play all their careers in our reserve team. They should be staking a claim for a first-team place.

'After a performance like that we will assess who we think can push on and look at those who will move on. There will be repercussions because it simply wasn't good enough.'

The first casualty of that evening was full-back Adam Yates, who was loaned out to Halifax. Only a brief flirtation with the substitutes bench against Bradford City and Mansfield in last season's LDV Vans Trophy was evidence of his time as a professional with us.

Mark Roberts also joined Leek Town on an extended loan period but that was for very different reasons. The Northwich-based defender has every chance of making it as a professional and was loaned out to Neil Baker's former club and then Vauxhall Motors as part of his development. His performances in non-league football earned rave reviews.

Another player making encouraging progress was Welshman David Vaughan, whose early season form at left-back and then on the left-hand side of midfield saw him called up for his country's crucial European Championship play-off against Russia.

Although only a squad member, it was a truly memorable experience for the Crewe youngster who was seen singing the national anthem on the television behind manager Mark Hughes in the return leg at the Millennium Stadium in Cardiff. Sadly, the Welsh lost 1–0 on aggregate and narrowly missed out on their first major finals since the World Cup finals of 1958.

If that wasn't hard enough to stomach for Vaughany, he injured his knee just before half time in the game at Norwich and surgery meant he would miss the next two and a half months of the season. It was a blow for our plans, especially as new acquisition Anthony Tonkin had just begun to settle into the left-back position following his move from Stockport.

Billy Jones and Stephen Foster surround Norwich's on-loan striker Peter Crouch at Carrow Road.

Saturday 1 November 2003 – 3.00pm- Gresty Road– Att: 7,091

Crewe Alexandra 1 Reading 0

S. Jones 15

Crewe Alexandra

1	Clayton Ince
2	David Wright
3	Richard Walker
4	Kenny Lunt
6	Stephen Foster
7	Neil Sorvel
9	Steve Jones
10	Dean Ashton
11	David Vaughan
16	Anthony Tonkin
19	Justin Cochrane

Substitutes

13	Ademole Bankole
14	Ben Rix
20	Allan Smart
28	Andrew Barrowman
29	Billy Jones

Referee

Mr Eddie Ilderton (Tyne & Wear)

Reading

1	Marcus Hahnemann
3	Nicholas Shorey
7	Scott Murray
8	Adrian Williams
10	Nicky Forster
11	Andy Hughes
14	Steven Sidwell
15	James Harper
16	Ivar Ingimarsson
17	John Salako
25	Ricky Newman

Substitutes

2	Graeme Murty (Newman 56)
4	Kevin Watson
9	Shaun Goater (Salako 79)
20	Bas Savage (Murray 88)
21	Jamie Ashdown

MATCH REPORT

A juggle of formation by Dario Gradi brought its rewards at Gresty Road as Steve Jones moved back into the attack from the wing and duly scored a superb goal to sink play-off hopefuls Reading.

The Alex boss left on-loan forward Andrew Barrowman out of his starting line up and recalled Anthony Tonkin to left back, which allowed David Vaughan to play in midfield, thus freeing Jones to use his pace up front.

And Jones exploited the role to the full to score Crewe's winner after just 15 minutes, with an assured finish that showed just how far the Northern Ireland international has come since joining the club from non-league Leigh RMI.

Jones's sixth goal of the season was enough to separate the two sides and was taken with some aplomb as he rounded Royals 'keeper Marcus Hahnemann before sliding the ball into the net from the tightest of angles after being slipped behind the Reading defence by Justin Cochrane's excellent pass.

Nicky Forster was Reading's greatest threat and three times in the first half he should have tested Clayton Ince from inside the box but instead missed the target to add to the visitors' frustrations.

In the second half, Reading certainly came back into the game and, on occasions, threatened to overwhelm Crewe's youngsters. But the Alex defence was rock solid throughout the second 45 minutes and even the late introduction of veteran striker Shaun Goater couldn't force an equaliser for Steve Coppell's team.

Dario's Comments

'Steve's goal was a great finish and he could have scored another one at the end. We have been telling him that if he gets a chance then he should go past the goalkeeper because he has the pace to do it.'

Steve Coppell's Comments

'I thought we deserved a point from the game. But their goal was a terrific finish from a tight angle. They make excellent runs and they're superbly schooled. All credit to Dario.'

The Sun

Dario Gradi reckons his team has got six-appeal after a hard-fought win. The Alex are now just four points off a play-off spot after Steve Jones shot down Reading. And they are closing on the top six all the time after stretching their unbeaten run to five.

The Daily Express

Dario Gradi believes David Wright is ready for the Premiership after hitting the best form of his career. The stand-in captain was an inspirational figure as Crewe took their unbeaten run to five games against promotion-fancied Reading thanks to a goal from Steve Jones.

Kenny Lunt attempts to block a cross from Reading's John Salako.

David Vaughan bursts past Ricky Newman.

Sheffield United 2   Crewe Alexandra 0

Armstrong 21
Lester (penalty) 74

Sheffield United

25	Paul Gerrard
2	Rob Kozluk
3	Chris Armstrong
5	Chris Morgan
8	Stuart McCall
9	Ashley Ward
11	Jack Lester
16	Peter Ndlovu
17	Phil Jagielka
18	Michael Tonge
22	Alan Wright

Substitutes

4	Nick Montgomery
10	Paul Peschisolido (Lester 79)
12	Andy Parkinson (Ndlovu 79)
14	Wayne Allison
24	Mike Whitlow

Referee

Mr M. Cooper (Walsall)

Crewe Alexandra

1	Clayton Ince
2	David Wright
3	Richard Walker
4	Kenny Lunt
6	Stephen Foster
7	Neil Sorvel
9	Steve Jones
10	Dean Ashton
11	David Vaughan
16	Anthony Tonkin
19	Justin Cochrane

Substitutes

13	Ademole Bankole
14	Ben Rix (Vaughan 71)
20	Allan Smart (Lunt 80)
28	Andrew Barrowman
29	Billy Jones (Walker 68)

MATCH REPORT

A disallowed goal, a fluke goal and an unbelievable penalty decision were the talking points of the game as Crewe's five-match unbeaten run ended at high flying Sheffield United.

The Alex had started the game 'resembling Arsenal at their slickest' according to one newspaper and the Blades were lucky to touch the ball in the opening 20 minutes, but once Chris Armstrong fortuitously put the home side in front a minute later, it was all about Neil Warnock's team.

By then though the Railwaymen had already seen a 'goal' chalked off after an eagle-eyed linesman adjudged Steve Jones to be offside in the ninth minute. David Vaughan had released the rampaging Anthony Tonkin down the left flank and when Jones tucked his cross past Paul Gerrard and into the net the Alex travelling faithful thought their side had a deserved lead. But the goal was ruled out by a linesman's flag – a decision which could be described as 'tight' at best.

Crewe continued to dominate though and the home fans were beginning to get restless when their opening goal came completely out of the blue. Clayton Ince's clearance went straight to veteran midfield man Stuart McCall and when the ball came into the box it hit Armstrong on the back of the head before spinning into Crewe's goal via the foot of the post.

Stephen Foster should have levelled the score minutes later when he somehow missed the target from close range following Kenny Lunt's free kick but in fairness the Blades were in charge for much of the game.

With only one goal in it though, Crewe were always in the game; that is until 16 minutes from time when the Alex fell foul of referee Mark Cooper for the second time in 12 months.

Dario's Comments
'That is the worst we have looked this season. I thought their forwards played well and caused us problems, but their opening goal was a bit of a fluke and the penalty was a ridiculous decision. I'm just glad it came in a game we deserved to be losing.'

Neil Warnock's Comments
'Crewe started the game like a side who were unbeaten in five matches. We really struggled to get the ball off them.'

The Guardian
One Crewe attack, which would have graced Arsenal at their slickest, sadly ended with David Vaughan shooting wide of the post.

The Daily Mirror
Crewe were brought back down to earth with a bump as their unbeaten run came to an end at Bramall Lane. Dario Gradi's side suffered their first defeat in six games against a Sheffield United outfit that put their recent woes behind them.

The Walsall-based official had sent off Richard Walker at Wigan 12 months earlier during our promotion campaign, and again gave a ridiculous decision against us as Neil Sorvel was adjudged to have handled in the box after the ball bounced up and hit his arm after a challenge with McCall.

Jack Lester stepped up to slot the penalty home to ensure United took all the spoils.

Despite the defeat, 16-year-old Billy Jones's 30-minute second-half display certainly raised a few eyebrows as he superbly marshalled former Crewe man Ashley Ward.

Rich Walker is not fooled by Jack Lester's tricky at Bramall Lane.

Jack Lester goes tumbling under a challenge from Stephen Foster and David Vaughan.

Saturday 8 November 2003 – 3pm – Priestfield Stadium – Att: 6,923

Gillingham 2 Crewe Alexandra 0

Shaw 64
Spiller 70

Gillingham

13	Jason Brown
2	Nyron Nosworthy
3	John Hills
4	Paul Smith
5	Barry Ashby
7	Nicky Southall
8	Andy Hessenthaler
10	Paul Shaw
22	Danny Spiller
26	David Perpetuini
29	Mamady Sidibe

Substitutes

11	Tommy Johnson
12	Bertrand Bossu
16	Richard Rose
17	Andrew Crofts
20	Kevin James (Hessenthaler 86)

Referee

Mr P. Taylor (Cheshunt)

Crewe Alexandra

1	Clayton Ince
2	David Wright
4	Kenny Lunt
6	Stephen Foster
7	Neil Sorvel
9	Steve Jones
10	Dean Ashton
11	David Vaughan
16	Anthony Tonkin
18	Chris McCready
19	Justin Cochrane

Substitutes

13	Ademole Bankole
14	Ben Rix (Sorvel 45)
17	James Robinson (Jones 83)
20	Allan Smart (Cochrane 80)
29	Billy Jones

MATCH REPORT

Kenny Lunt saw red for the first time in his career as Crewe crashed to their second 2–0 defeat in four days.

Lunt was dismissed late in the second half after an unsightly incident with Gillingham player-manager Andy Hessenthaler and his early bath capped a miserable afternoon for the Alex in Kent.

Referee Mr Taylor handed Crewe's playmaking midfield man his second yellow card in the second half after he reacted badly to a late tackle from Hessenthaler, right in front of the dug-outs, and Dario Gradi later described him as 'silly' for getting involved.

Chris McCready replaced Richard Walker in the Alex starting line-up in the only change to the side that lost at Sheffield United, but Crewe never really got going against the Gills, who created and ultimately scored the better chances.

After a goalless first half, in which neither side really looked like breaking the deadlock, Gillingham started the second period on top and took the lead on 64 minutes through Paul Shaw.

The lively forward made it 1–0 after Hessenthaler beat Ben Rix in a challenge outside the box and accurately crossed into the danger zone to give Shaw an easy opportunity, which he coolly tucked away.

Six minutes later it was all over as the home side scored a cracking goal in a move that carved Crewe's defence wide open. The excellent Nyron Nosworthy created the chance with an incisive run and cross to the left of the Alex penalty area, and young midfielder Danny Spiller did the rest with a superb volley that flew into Clayton Ince's net.

Any lingering hopes of a comeback were quickly extinguished by Lunt's red card and Crewe were fortunate not to lose by an even bigger margin when Paul Smith's thunderbolt rattled the cross bar in the dying minutes.

Dario's Comments
'Kenny and Hessenthaler were stupid. Kenny objected to the tackle and when you are on the floor like that you are liable to do something stupid and he did. They were both silly to get involved in something like that.'

Andy Hessenthaler's Comments
'At half time 0–0 wasn't the right score because I thought we should have gone in leading the game. But we upped the tempo in the second half and deserved to win the game.'

The Daily Express
Paul Shaw's fifth goal of the season, along with an unstoppable header from Danny Spiller from eight yards left Clayton Ince with no chance of keeping the visitors in the hunt.

The Sunday Sentinel
Crewe's miserable afternoon at the Priestfield Stadium was rounded off by Kenny Lunt's dismissal. The midfielder emerged from a sea of arms and legs with Gills player-manager Andy Hessenthaler and was promptly despatched down the tunnel by referee Paul Taylor.

Dean Ashton tracks Gillingham's John Hills.

Steve Jones wins an aerial duel with Barry Ashby.

Crewe Alexandra 3 Sunderland 0

Ashton 53
S. Jones 55, 63

Crewe Alexandra

1	Clayton Ince
2	David Wright
6	Stephen Foster
9	Steve Jones
10	Dean Ashton
11	David Vaughan
14	Ben Rix
16	Anthony Tonkin
18	Chris McCready
19	Justin Cochrane
29	Billy Jones

Substitutes

5	Adie Moses
13	Ademole Bankole
15	Luke Varney
17	James Robinson
20	Allan Smart

Referee

Mr C.J. Foy (St Helens)

Sunderland

1	Mart Poom
2	Stephen Wright
3	George McCartney
8	Jeff Whitley
10	Marcus Stewart
11	Tommy Smith
19	Alan Quinn
22	Joachim Bjorklund
24	Stewart Downing
25	Colin Healy
33	Julio Arca

Substitutes

6	Ben Clark (Stewart 83)
13	Michael Ingham
14	Michael Proctor (Quinn 70)
21	Paul Thirwell
23	Chris Black

MATCH REPORT

After surviving a first half onslaught from the visitors, the Alex produced a wonderful performance after the break to stun Sunderland and run out 3–0 winners at Gresty Road.

Mick McCarthy's side were left utterly shell-shocked by three goals in 20 minutes in the second period as Dean Ashton's header and a well-taken brace by Steve Jones continued Crewe's superb run of form in South Cheshire.

Having impressed during bit-part roles when coming off the bench over the previous few games, Dario Gradi handed 16-year-old Billy Jones his full debut in central midfield, in place of the suspended Kenny Lunt, and the youngster was one of many star performers.

Chris McCready gets to grips with Sunderland's Tommy Smith.

In the first half though it was Sunderland who were on top as they passed the ball around better than any other side at the Alexandra Stadium this season. But the Black Cats' finishing in front of goal was far from impressive as Jeff Whitley and Tommy Smith both missed good chances and Clayton Ince saved comfortably from Stephen Wright.

Dario's Comments
'It was an excellent performance because Sunderland are a very good side who pass the ball about well. In the second half we produced that bit of quality that we know we can produce and we got the goals.'

Mick McCarthy's Comments
'It's bemusing to play as well as we did in the first half then lose 3–0. It looks like a spanking but it was anything but. They had goalscorers on the day that were better than ours. There's no point creating chances and not scoring.'

News of the World
Three goals in nine minutes stunned the Black Cats, who had looked like cruising it. The quick-fire triple – two from Steve Jones and one from strike partner Dean Ashton – early in the second half killed off the Wearsiders.

Dario in *The Times*
'Somebody said to me on Friday, it could be a great day if England win the World Cup and Crewe beat Sunderland and I think you'd have got good money on both happening!'

Crewe celebrate Dean Ashton's headed opener against the Black Cats.

Sunderland's best chance though fell to former Ipswich front man Marcus Stewart. Ince could only parry Stewart Downing's fierce drive and Stewart reacted quickest to the rebound only to see his effort hit the foot of the post.

After the break the visitors' goalscoring troubles were the last thing on their minds as the Railwaymen raced into a three-goal lead.

The Alex were in front after just eight minutes and owed much to the strength of their youngest player for the goal. Billy Jones brushed off the challenge of Whitley in midfield before releasing David Vaughan on the left, and his pin-point cross was well converted by Ashton's head.

Billy was involved again two minutes later as Crewe made it 2–0, but it was Justin Cochrane with the final pass to Steve Jones who elegantly lifted the ball over Mart Poom for another expert finish.

Within eight minutes the game was dead and buried as the Alex struck again to leave the visitors in tatters. This time it was a deadly set-piece routine that caught out the Wearsiders as Stephen Foster won the flick on and Chris McCready sent the ball back into the danger zone. The ever-alert Steve Jones pounced on it like a true penalty-box poacher and, although his first effort clattered the crossbar, he followed up immediately to find the target from close range.

Norwich City 1   Crewe Alexandra 0

Huckerby 39

Norwich City

1	Robert Green
3	Adam Drury
4	Malky Mackay
5	Craig Fleming
6	Darren Huckerby
7	Phil Mulryne
8	Gary Holt
17	Marc Edworthy
18	Paul McVeigh
22	Ian Henderson
25	Peter Crouch

Substitutes

9	Iwan Roberts
11	Jim Brennan (McVeigh 67)
12	Paul Crichton
20	Damien Francis
23	Ryan Jarvis (Henderson 83)

Referee

Andy Penn (West Midlands)

Crewe Alexandra

1	Clayton Ince
2	David Wright
6	Stephen Foster
9	Steve Jones
10	Dean Ashton
11	David Vaughan
14	Ben Rix
16	Anthony Tonkin
18	Chris McCready
19	Justin Cochrane
29	Billy Jones

Substitutes

3	Richard Walker
4	Kenny Lunt (Vaughan 45)
13	Ademole Bankole
15	Luke Varney (B. Jones 45)
20	Allan Smart

MATCH REPORT

Despite a spirited second-half display at Carrow Road, the Alex slipped to defeat against the league leaders thanks to Darren Huckerby's first half strike.

In truth it was no more than the home side deserved, but the Alex were in the game right up until the final whistle after a much-improved second-half showing which tested Nigel Worthington's side to the full.

Dario opted to name an unchanged side from the one that had beaten Sunderland the week before and surprisingly resisted the temptation to restore Kenny Lunt to the starting line up following his return from suspension. But Crewe were second best in the first 45 minutes as the Canaries signalled their intentions early on, with a Paul McVeigh shot in the first few seconds which was well saved by Clayton Ince, although it was on-loan duo Huckerby and Peter Crouch who caused most of the Alex's problems.

Huckerby had a decent penalty appeal, following a challenge by Stephen Foster, waved away in the 18th minute, and although the former Leeds United and Coventry City striker wasted a number of gilt-edged opportunities, he was a constant thorn in Crewe's side.

After Ince had produced superb saves to deny McVeigh and Crouch in separate attacks, Huckerby finally found the target seven minutes before the break.

Gary Holt headed Phil Mulryne's cross into Huckerby's path and he took a touch before curling it beyond Ince and in at the far post.

After hanging on for so long the goal seemed inevitable, but after the break Crewe could have snatched an equaliser after a lively

Dario's Comments
'I thought we were fortunate to go in at the break with us only one goal behind because they created a lot of chances and it could have been more. We attacked much better in the second half without being good enough to get that goal.'

Nigel Worthington's Comments
'I'm delighted. I thought our overall play was excellent and we could have scored four or five. The boys were positive from minute one and it was a good three points.'

The Sun
Norwich fans know what they want for Christmas – on-loan stars Darren Huckerby and Peter Crouch on permanent deals.

Daily Mirror
It's not a question of whether Norwich can afford to sign Darren Huckerby and Peter Crouch – it's a question of whether they can afford NOT to sign them.

Match-winner Darren Huckerby takes on
our own Chris McCready.

second 45 minutes. Dario introduced Lunt and
Luke Varney in place of the injured David
Vaughan and Billy Jones and the alterations to
personnel seemed to work wonders.

Varney came close within minutes of his
introduction and Dean Ashton brought an
excellent save from Robert Green soon after. Ben
Rix also went close while Steve Jones was denied
on two occasions, once by Green and once by
defender Marc Edworthy, but that elusive
equaliser never came.

It was a disappointment to the tremendous
250 following supporters, who endured
horrendous conditions on an open terrace to
support their team.

Vaughany skips away from Ian
Henderson's sliding tackle.

December Review

The final month of what proved to be a very successful year for Crewe Alexandra saw Billy Jones prematurely end the Goal of the Season competition against Wigan Athletic. His spectacular volley from Kenny Lunt's corner will remain long in the memory and is arguably one of the club's greatest ever goals. Not bad for a young 16-year-old making only the sixth start of a promising career!

December also saw a vast improvement in our away results. Our first-ever win at Selhurst Park over Crystal Palace was followed up with gutsy draws at the then league leaders West Bromwich Albion and Preston North End.

It was an indifferent period at home, with Gillingham obtaining a deserved point thanks to David Perpetuini's long-range effort and a vastly improving Wigan side claiming all three points in a five-goal thriller just before Christmas.

The players bounced back from that disappointment with a fine 3–1 win over Burnley on Boxing Day. Steve Jones was on target twice with his strike partner Dean Ashton claiming the other in front of a healthy crowd of 8,512.

The first team were drawn against non-league outfit Telford United in the Third Round of the FA Cup and would face Mick Jones's experienced side in the first week of January at the Alexandra Stadium.

The club's injury nightmare became

Adie Moses and Crewe celebrated an historic first-ever win at Crystal Palace.

increasingly worse over the hectic festive period with no less than 10 first-team performers ruled out at one stage for various reasons. Club captain Dave Brammer underwent surgery on his troublesome groin strain in Bolton and a return to action before the end of the season was a welcome boost to Dario Gradi, who had originally written him off for the season.

Ben Rix joined Crewe's growing injury list in December.

The unfortunate Chris McCready also spent more time on the sidelines due to various niggling injuries and he was restricted to just 15 starting appearances. With Rich Walker and Adie Moses also struggling to get a consistent run of games under their belts, the club's newly elected skipper David Wright switched into the centre of the defence.

With injuries taking their toll, manager Dario Gradi was forced to include youngsters Luke Varney, Michael Higdon, Ian Jeffs, Gary Roberts, Paul Edwards and James Robinson in his plans more often than not. In fact four of those players made their senior debuts during the festive period.

The club's Youth Team progressed to the fourth round of the competition with a 1–0 win over Brentford. England Under-17 international Gary Roberts scored the only goal of the game at the Alexandra Stadium to set up a difficult tie at non-league Cirencester Town.

With the transfer window rapidly approaching for Premier League clubs, a host of clubs were linked with possible moves for David Wright and Dean Ashton, but thankfully for us nothing was forthcoming in terms of concrete offers.

Dario did admit that Wright, 23, was ready for the challenge of the Premier League, and even allowed the versatile defender to spend a day training with troubled Leeds United. Warrington-born Wright certainly didn't let the speculation bother him and continued to perform consistently well in the back four. 'Since I was about 17 I have been linked with various clubs but nothing has ever happened,' said David. 'But since the last time with the Fulham thing and with Leeds, which came close but never happened, you just have to get on with things. I believe in fate and what will be will be. If something happens then brilliant because everyone wants to go as far as they can in the game. But until anything happens, I'm not really paying any attention to speculation.'

Crewe Alexandra 1 Gillingham 1

S. Jones 11   Perpetuini 50

Crewe Alexandra

1	Clayton Ince
2	David Wright
4	Kenny Lunt
6	Stephen Foster
9	Steve Jones
10	Dean Ashton
14	Ben Rix
16	Anthony Tonkin
18	Chris McCready
19	Justin Cochrane
29	Billy Jones

Substitutes

3	Richard Walker (Rix 59)
5	Adie Moses (Walker 89)
13	Ademole Bankole
15	Luke Varney
20	Allan Smart

Referee
Mr G. Cain (Bootle)

Gillingham

13	Jason Brown
2	Nyron Nosworthy
3	John Hills
4	Paul Smith
6	Ian Cox
7	Nicky Southall
10	Paul Shaw
18	Chris Hope
20	Kevin James
26	David Perpetuini
29	Mamady Sidibe

Substitutes

5	Barry Ashby
15	Mark Saunders
16	Richard Rose
22	Danny Spiller
27	Jones Awuah

MATCH REPORT

Crewe faced Andy Hessenthaler's Gillingham side for the second time in a month on a bitterly cold day in South Cheshire. Steve Jones warmed up the masses with his ninth goal of the season after just 11 minutes – but we were unable to preserve the lead with David Perpetuini netting from distance five minutes after the interval.

Crewe were without David Vaughan, who had injured his knee at Carrow Road the week before. Ben Rix came in on the left-hand side with youngster Billy Jones retaining his place in the centre of midfield. Kenny Lunt returned to the side after being named as a substitute at Norwich following his red card away at Gillingham.

Jones gave Crewe the lead after Gills 'keeper Jason Brown failed to get any real distance on a punch. Dean Ashton had forced the error by pressuring the 'keeper following David Wright's accurately struck free-kick into the box and Jonah was well placed to drill home the opener. It was his third goal on the trot in home matches.

In reply, Paul Shaw forced Clayton Ince into two smart saves and full-back Nyron Nosworthy was a thorn in our side with his raids down the right flank. Former Blackpool defender John Hills also wasted a glorious chance after a corner had fallen invitingly at his feet in the box.

Ashton had an opportunity to make it 2–0 before the interval but Brown redeemed himself by making a decent save in a one-on-one situation.

Five minutes into the second half Ince was caught cold by a wonderful strike from Perpetuini. The former Watford midfielder unleashed a ferocious shot from 30 yards that dipped at just the right moment for the visitors.

Dario Gradi's Comments
'I think we did well to get a point in the end. Gillingham were a good passing side and we put more pressure on them than we did at their place. But in the end it should have been 0–0 because both goalkeepers made mistakes. Their goalkeeper made a cock-up for our goal and our goalkeeper made a cock-up for theirs.'

Andy Hessenthaler's Comments
'I'm not being critical of the team or the performance but sometimes you need that 'fox in the box' as they say – to bang it in the net. I thought we were the best team in the second half but we couldn't produce the quality in attack.'

The Times
David Perpetuini's second-half wonder goal ended Crewe Alexandra's run of four consecutive home wins. Crewe had taken the lead against the run of play in the 11th minute through Steve Jones after Jason Brown had dropped a cross.

News Of The World
Crewe boss Dario Gradi was left fuming after his 'keeper Clayton Ince gifted Gillingham a point. The Trinidad star simply waved David Perpetuini's long-range strike into his net.

Rix limped out of the game with a broken toe and then we also lost Rich Walker with an ankle injury after he had blocked Shaw on the edge of the box. The treatment room was getting busier by the game!

Paul Smith had a late chance to win it for the visitors while Ashton was just wide at the other end with time running out. But it was an excellent point won.

Steve Jones celebrates the opening goal against Gillingham.

The Advance Personnel Stand erupts after Jonah's goal.

Tuesday 9 December 2003 – 8pm – Selhurst Park – Att: 12,259

Crystal Palace 1 Crewe Alexandra 3

Butterfield 78

Ashton 8, 86
Varney 16

Crystal Palace

25	Thomas Myhre
2	Curtis Fleming
4	Danny Butterfield
5	Kit Symons
9	Dougie Freedman
10	Shaun Derry
11	Neil Shipperley
15	Aki Riihilahti
18	Gary Borrowdale
19	Rob Edwards
22	Wayne Routledge

Substitutes

3	Danny Granville
13	Cedric Berthelin
14	Ben Watson
16	Tommy Black (Fleming 72)
17	Michael Hughes

Referee
P. Joslin (Newark)

Crewe Alexandra

1	Clayton Ince
2	David Wright
4	Kenny Lunt
6	Stephen Foster
9	Steve Jones
10	Dean Ashton
15	Luke Varney
16	Anthony Tonkin
18	Chris McCready
19	Justin Cochrane
29	Billy Jones

Substitutes

5	Adie Moses (McCready 82)
13	Ademole Bankole
17	James Robinson
20	Allan Smart (Varney 79)
26	Michael Higdon (Ashton 88)

MATCH REPORT

Dean Ashton inspired Crewe Alexandra to our first-ever win at Selhurst Park and only our second away victory of the season. The Swindon-born forward scored once in each half to pile on the misery for managerless Crystal Palace. Luke Varney sandwiched his first senior goal in between Ashton's brace, as Dario Gradi altered the tactics to suit the players he had available.

Varney, making his full league debut, and Steve Jones operated as wingers with Kenny Lunt pushing forward to support Ashton. It worked a treat with Crewe establishing a two-goal lead within the first 20 minutes.

Ashton's first goal of the evening arrived on eight minutes after he turned sharply on the edge of the Palace box before firing low past Thomas Myhre. Varney added a well-taken second eight minutes later after he held off the intentions of Gary Borrowdale inside the six-yard box to round off a slick passing move from the Alex.

With Lunt relishing the freedom of his new role and Palace unable to cope with the pace of our wingers, Crewe produced one of most impressive attacking displays of the season.

Myhre was forced to push over a Lunt free kick before Stephen Foster missed a great chance to seal the points after a Lunt corner had invitingly dropped at the defender's feet.

As you would expect, the home side gave it a real go in the second half and Wayne Routledge and Neil Shipperley came close before Danny Butterfield's lifeline finish on 78 minutes.

Never ones for doing it the easy way, it looked liked being a tense finish to a game Crewe had controlled from the first whistle. Thankfully, with just four minutes to go, Ashton stole a yard inside the Palace box to head home a Kenny Lunt free kick and secure a long-awaited away win.

Dario Gradi's Comments
'It is a terrific result for us because this is only our second away win of the season. I'm pleased for the players, the supporters and myself because it has been a long time coming and we will all enjoy the long trip home.'

Kit Symons's Comments
'We were poor in the first half and found ourselves two goals behind fairly early. We organised at half-time and I thought we were a lot better and made a game of it, but the third goal killed us off.'

The Crewe Chronicle
Midfield man Kenny Lunt played a starring role with assists with all three goals. Varney was given a full debut in place of Ben Rix as the Crewe manager fielded an attacking 4–3–3 formation.

The Sentinel
Dario Gradi turned back the years to 1997 as a change of system earned Crewe their first ever win at Crystal Palace. Faced with an injury crisis, the Alex manager hedged his bets and abandoned the 4–4–2 formation, which away from home has failed to match some roaring successes at the Alexandra Stadium.

Dean Ashton celebrates the first of his two goals at Selhurst Park.

West Bromwich Albion 2 Crewe Alexandra 2

Haas 7
Gregan 72

S. Jones 18
Wright 45

West Bromwich Albion

1	Russell Hoult
2	Bernt Haas
4	James O'Connor
10	Andy Johnson
12	Scott Dobie
14	Sean Gregan
15	Rob Hulse
18	Jason Koumas
24	Thomas Gaardsoe
25	Joost Volmer
33	Paul Robinson

Substitutes

3	Neil Clement
19	Lee Hughes (Dobie 63)
20	Artim Sakiri (O'Connor 50)
21	Joe Murphy (Gk)
22	James Chambers

Referee

G. Hegley (Bishop's Stortford)

Crewe Alexandra

1	Clayton Ince
2	David Wright
4	Kenny Lunt
6	Stephen Foster
9	Steve Jones
10	Dean Ashton
15	Luke Varney
16	Anthony Tonkin
18	Chris McCready
19	Justin Cochrane
29	Billy Jones

Substitutes

5	Adie Moses (B. Jones 43)
13	Ademole Bankole
17	James Robinson
20	Allan Smart
26	Michael Higdon

MATCH REPORT

Crewe Alexandra claimed another impressive away point against the then-league leaders West Bromwich Albion. All the pre-match talk concerned the fact that old boy Rob Hulse was facing his home-town club for the first time following his summer £1 million move to the Hawthorns.

In the first 20 minutes the home side threw everything at us and it was no great surprise that they took an early lead through full-back Bernt Haas. Clayton Ince fumbled a Jason Koumas free kick onto the post and Haas was given the easy task of tapping home the opener after seven minutes.

Under the cosh, Ince recovered well to save from Andy Johnson and Thomas Gaardsoe before Stephen Foster blocked a goalbound effort from James O'Connor.

Then against the run of play Crewe equalised through Steve Jones. He side-footed home a Kenny Lunt corner to level things up after a hectic 18 minutes.

A frustrated Hulse was cautioned for a lunging tackle on David Wright before Luke Varney had a decent opening to give us the lead.

Paul Robinson then struck the inside of Clayton Ince's post before we lost the outstanding Billy Jones after an accidental clash of heads involving Hulse. Adie Moses replaced him in the heart of the defence, with Chris McCready switching to right-back and captain Wright pushed into midfield. The reshuffle certainly paid off with Wright latching onto a Dean Ashton knock down to give us a half-time lead.

At the start of the second half, Varney went awfully close to extending our lead but he just failed to reach Anthony Tonkin's low cross.

Following that scare, West Brom began to regain their composure and midfielder

Luke Varney and Sean Gregan both leap into the air at the Hawthorns.

Koumas became more influential. The Welshman forced Ince into a smart save before creating Hulse's best chance from a corner. Ince tipped his mate's point-blank header over the bar.

It looked as though Crewe were capable of holding out for all three points but with just 13 minutes to go, captain Sean Gregan was allowed to run unimpeded into the Crewe box and Robinson picked him out splendidly to save the table-topping Baggies.

The introduction of the fit-again Adie Moses saw goalscorer David Wright switch into midfield.

Saturday 20 December 2003 –3pm – Gresty Road – Att: 7,837

Crewe Alexandra 2 Wigan Athletic 3

B. Jones 10
S. Jones 16

McCulloch 8
De Vos 20
Bullard 80

Crewe Alexandra

1	Clayton Ince
2	David Wright
4	Kenny Lunt
6	Stephen Foster
9	Steve Jones
10	Dean Ashton
15	Luke Varney
16	Anthony Tonkin
19	Justin Cochrane
26	Michael Higdon
29	Billy Jones

Substitutes

13	Ademole Bankole
17	James Robinson (Varney 81)
20	Allan Smart
21	Paul Edwards
28	Gary Roberts

Referee

L. Cable (Woking)

Wigan Athletic

1	John Filan
2	Paul Mitchell
5	Jason De Vos
7	Andy Liddell
9	Nathan Ellington
10	Lee McCulloch
18	Jason Jarrett
19	Nicky Eaden
20	Gary Teale
21	Jimmy Bullard
24	Alan Rogers

Substitutes

8	Neil Roberts
12	Michael Flynn
13	Gary Walsh
14	Jamie Lawrence (Liddell 67)
26	Leighton Baines (Rogers 27)

MATCH REPORT

Horrendous torrential rain and swirling wind did not prevent both sides from playing some very watchable football. Wigan Athletic won it in the end with Jimmy Bullard unleashing an unstoppable shot with 10 minutes to go, but that goal didn't even come close to rivalling Billy Jones's first senior goal for Crewe.

An outrageous set-piece corner routine saw Kenny Lunt pick out the unmarked youngster on the edge of the box and he quite simply stepped forward and lashed it into the top corner of John Filan's net. That memorable 10th-minute strike also cancelled out Lee McCulloch's opener two minutes earlier. The Wigan forward had turned in a Gary Teale cross to give the visitors the lead.

Crewe then took the lead in the 16th minute when Steve Jones calmly slotted home from an acute angle after Wright's clever pass had put him clean through.

In a topsy-turvy opening, Kenny Lunt and then Bullard both went close with free kicks before the powerful Jason De Vos drew his side level on 20 minutes. The Canadian defender was in the thick of it to convert a Nicky Eaden cross from close range.

The game could have gone either way with winger Teale impressing for Wigan and Michael Higdon making his full debut for the club in place of the injured Chris McCready.

With an entertaining half coming to a close, Andy Liddell couldn't quite stretch enough to reach an Ellington cross before Dean Ashton was unlucky in stoppage time after a mazy run.

With both sides searching for the advantage of that third goal, Ellington dragged another shot wide of the target before McCullogh headed wide of the mark after a centre from Teale.

In reply, Crewe's best effort saw Steve Jones

Dario's Comments
'It's one I have seen on TV somewhere and we've been practising it, but Billy has gone absolutely nowhere near to finding the target. We'd almost eliminated it but Billy has a tremendous strike and I told him to just hit the target.'

Paul Jewell's Comments
'It's a great win for us after what has been a hard week with us losing Geoff Horsfield to West Brom. It was a magnificent effort from everyone involved and though it was a tight game, I felt we deserved the victory in the end as we did look the more dangerous of the two sides.'

The Daily Star
Golf nut Jimmy Bullard hit the perfect shot to keep Wigan on course for a promotion push.
The midfielder hopes to swap his football boots for golf clubs when his football career is over, but that won't be for a while. With the game locked at 2–2 for an hour, Bullard cut in from the left to hit a 30-yard screamer past Clayton Ince.

Daily Telegraph
It was ironic that while Dario Gradi has produced an endless line of talent at Gresty Road, Wigan marched back into the first division promotion race with a virtuoso goal from the type of player typical of a Gradi signing.

Justin Cochrane and
Jason Jarrett challenge
for possession in the air.

acrobatically reach an Anthony Tonkin cross but Filan did well to back-pedal and tip the effort over his bar.

Cochrane collected a costly fifth booking of the season for a foul on Bullard and that meant he would miss our FA Cup tie against Telford United in two weeks time.

The game could really have gone either way but a moment of individual ability from Bullard claimed all three points for the Latics. Bullard's dipping drive gave Ince little chance of saving it. Crewe continued to press for an equaliser and it looked as though Ashton had saved us at the death only for his goal to be ruled out for offside. The match video indicated it was a harsh decision.

Crewe Alexandra 3 Burnley 1

Ashton 57
S. Jones 55, 90

Blake (pen) 88

Crewe Alexandra

1	Clayton Ince
2	David Wright
4	Kenny Lunt
6	Stephen Foster
9	Steve Jones
10	Dean Ashton
15	Luke Varney
16	Anthony Tonkin
19	Justin Cochrane
26	Michael Higdon
29	Billy Jones

Substitutes

13	Ademole Bankole
17	James Robinson (Cochrane 53)
20	Allan Smart
21	Paul Edwards
28	Gary Roberts (Varney 82)

Referee

T. Parkes (Birmingham)

Burnley

1	Brian Jensen
3	Mohammed Camara
4	Paul Weller
6	Graham Branch
7	Glen Little
8	Robert Blake
10	Ian Moore
12	Tony Grant
15	Dean West
17	Arthur Gnohere
20	Richard Chaplow

Substitutes

2	Lee Roche
14	Mark McGregor (West 71)
16	Luke Chadwick (Little 16)
21	Matthew O'Neill
18	James McEveley (Chaplow 59)

MATCH REPORT

Crewe Alexandra recorded their eighth home success of the season with a fairly comfortable win over Burnley on Boxing Day. Strike duo Dean Ashton and Steve Jones continued their impressive form with the decisive goals in the Cheshire drizzle to push Crewe into the top half of the table.

With the injury list growing by the game, manager Dario Gradi had to select a side without 10 possible first-team players. Therefore, there was another chance for youngsters Michael Higdon, Billy Jones and Luke Varney. 16-year-old Gary Roberts also came off the bench to mark his senior debut in the Crewe midfield.

Both sides had early chances with Clayton Ince tipping over an effort from Glen Little (who would soon withdraw with a hamstring strain) before Varney forced Burnley's 'keeper Brian Jensen into his first save of the afternoon.

Burnley continuously tried their luck from distance with Richard Chaplow, Graham Branch and Mo Camara all having efforts saved by Ince.

Steve Jones then went close for Crewe on the half-an-hour mark before Ashton finally broke the stalemate seven minutes later. The England Under-21 forward turned sharply on a pass from Kenny Lunt before lashing home his 10th goal of the season.

Stan Ternent certainly stirred his Clarets in the dressing room and the visitors were rather unfortunate not to equalise during their best spell of the game. Stephen Foster did exceedingly well to clear an effort from Arthur

David Wright and Anthony Tonkin win this heading duel against Ian Moore during our Boxing Day win over Burnley.

Gnohere before the lively Robbie Blake tested our resolve with a couple of snapshots.

James Robinson replaced hamstring victim Justin Cochrane before we increased our advantage on 55 minutes. Burnley's centre-backs Branch and Gnohere made a right hash of attempting to deal with Ashton's lay-off, thus allowing Steve Jones to race clear and curl it past Jensen for 2–0.

Burnley were given a glimmer of hope when Anthony Tonkin was adjudged to have tripped Luke Chadwick in the area. Blake slotted home the penalty to increase the pressure slightly in the closing minutes. That pressure was eased when Steve Jones latched on to a Lunt through ball before calmly burying his 13th goal of the season. It was a nice way to celebrate Christmas.

Preston North End 0 Crewe Alexandra 0

Preston North End

40	Jonathan Gould
2	Graham Alexander
3	Brian O'Neil
4	Dickson Etuhu
5	Michael Jackson
9	Ricardo Fuller
11	David Healy
17	Eddie Lewis
18	Pawel Abbott
20	Chris Lucketti
22	Claude Davis

Substitutes

8	Lee Cartwright
13	Andrew Lonergan
24	Tyrone Mears
25	Richard Cresswell (Abbott 45)
26	Eric Skora (Etuhu 76)

Referee

R.Pearson (Peterlee)

Crewe Alexandra

1	Clayton Ince
2	David Wright
4	Kenny Lunt
6	Stephen Foster
9	Steve Jones
10	Dean Ashton
15	Luke Varney
16	Anthony Tonkin
19	Justin Cochrane
26	Michael Higdon
29	Billy Jones

Substitutes

13	Ademole Bankole
14	Ben Rix (Cochrane 89)
17	James Robinson
20	Allan Smart
28	Gary Roberts

MATCH REPORT

A successful 2003 ended with a hard-earned point at Preston's Deepdale Stadium. Despite the blank scoreline, it was still an entertaining affair with the major incident occurring in the final minute of play after Dean Ashton was adjudged to have handled a cross in the box. Thankfully for Crewe, goalkeeper Clayton Ince rose to the occasion to save Graham Alexander's well-struck penalty and preserve a precious point.

Billy Jones keeps Eddie Lewis at bay at Deepdale.

With numbers thin on the ground it was rather surprising that Dario was able to name an unchanged side for the third consecutive match. Justin Cochrane shook off his slight hamstring strain to retain his place in the side, while the fit-again Ben Rix was named in the

Dario's Comments

'I've been delighted with the Christmas we have had because I don't really like to talk about injuries but we've had our fair share and the positive thing this Christmas is that we have come through it with four points. Players like Michael Higdon, I wasn't sure about when I first played them and I'm still not totally sure about him but although he has a bit to do he played like a man today.'

Craig Brown's Comments

'We had enough chances to win the game and most notably we missed the penalty in the final minute. We are very disappointed to have only got a point at home, but on another day they could have snatched all the points themselves.'

The Daily Mirror

Clayton Ince made a dramatic penalty save in the final minute to secure a point for Crewe. The Trinidad and Tobago international saved Graham Alexander's spot kick after Dean Ashton had allegedly handled in the area.

The Daily Express

Crewe recorded only their eighth away point of the season with a spirited performance at Preston. Goalkeeper Clayton Ince was the hero of the day, saving Graham Alexander's last minute penalty.

squad for the first time since the home draw with Gillingham.

After a 15-minute delay due to traffic congestion, both sides had chances to win a flowing encounter. American Eddie Lewis whipped an early free-kick just wide of the target before David Wright courageously blocked shots from the highly-rated Ricardo Fuller and Pawel Abbot.

Dean Ashton registered Crewe's first real effort on goal following a clever interchange of passing involving Kenny Lunt and Steve Jones. Ashton's powerful hit was superbly tipped over by the agile Jonathan Gould. Jones then chanced his luck from 40 yards after spotting the Scottish goalkeeper slightly off his line. At the other end a resilient Crewe defence saw Stephen Foster make a superb recovery challenge on Abbot before the Preston midfielder tried to win his side a penalty by 'falling down' in a crowded penalty area.

Varney had a decent chance just after half-time but failed to connect with an Ashton cross and then Michael Higdon volleyed over from a set-piece corner routine. The game was finely poised going into the closing stages with both sides having enough chances to steal all three points. Lunt nearly capitalised on a poor clearance from Gould but his shot lacked direction while at the other end the referee waved away appeals for another penalty when Foster stole possession off Fuller's foot.

Steve Jones then forced Gould into a fine reaction save with a little over 15 minutes left when he headed a Billy Jones cross goalwards.

Just when it looked as though Crewe were holding on for a deserved point, referee Pearson surprised everyone by awarding that last-minute penalty. Ince managed to prevent Alexander's spot-kick and the right full-back made a mess of the rebound. Crewe had their deserved point.

January Review

It wasn't a winning start to 2004 for Crewe Alexandra as Telford United registered the upset of the FA Cup Third Round. Former Stoke and Port Vale striker Lee Mills headed the only goal of the game in the second minute to dump us out of the Cup at the first hurdle.

In truth, Crewe dominated from the moment Mills rose above Luke Varney

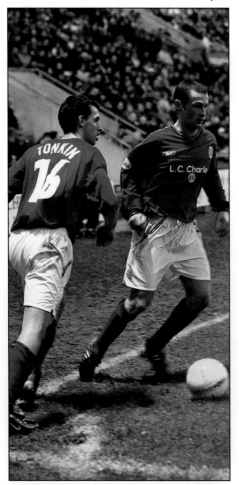

Tonks and Lunty activate a quick free kick against Telford United.

and Clayton Ince to head home the priceless winner, but we couldn't find the equaliser that would have led to a replay at their vastly improved Bucks Head Stadium.

Mick Jones had certainly done his homework, electing to nullify the creativeness of Kenny Lunt by ordering the experienced Fitzroy Simpson to marshal his every move. They also out-foxed us with one of our own trademark set-piece routines, the near-post corner. From then on, the non-leaguers defended resolutely and despite their own disappointment the Alex supporters applauded their efforts at the end of the game. Telford's reward was a home tie with eventual finalists Millwall.

A week later and the players bounced back with another home victory over struggling Wimbledon. Steve Jones was again on target and in doing so, propelled himself into the top 10 leading scorers in the First Division.

That proved to be our only points in January. A bizarre 6–4 defeat at Ipswich was followed a week later by an undeserved home defeat at the hands of Millwall. On-loan striker Daniele Dichio netted an injury-time winner after Andy Roberts had inadvertently deflected a Kenny Lunt free-kick past his own 'keeper to cancel out Dichio's first-half opener.

Dario revisited the transfer system after an attempted loan swoop for former player Mark Rivers was blocked by Norwich City. On the recommendation of Neil Baker, he chose to bring promising Irishman Eamon Zayed in on loan until the end of the season. The Bray Wanderers striker was given an extended opportunity to prove

The scoreboard at Portman Road says it all.

that he had enough ability to make the transformation from the First Division in Ireland to the First Division in England.

The decision to bring the Republic of Ireland Under-21 forward over proved to be a beneficial one because Dario then lost two of his covering forwards due to injury. Allan Smart needed knee surgery and was ruled out for the rest of the campaign and it was a similar tale for Luke Varney, who underwent an operation to correct a long-standing shoulder complaint. The former Quorn forward only returned for the last month of the season after being stretched off against Telford.

The club also welcomed back youngsters Ian Jeffs and Tom Betts from their time in Iceland with IBV. Due to FIFA regulations they had been unable to represent the club again until the transfer window reopened on 1 January. Jeffs went on to make his one and only appearance as a late substitute in the cup defeat to Telford before he was released to rejoin IBV.

Betts later went on loan to Vauxhall Motors to join fellow defender Mark Roberts,

who had impressed during his time at Leek Town. Other players moving on were Carl Frost, who signed on loan at Leek after being released, and goalkeeper Ademole Bankole, who went on a three-month loan to Barnet before being recalled due to a thigh injury to Clayton Ince.

Lee Bell prematurely returned from his season-long loan at Shrewsbury for personal reasons to boost the numbers in our injury-hit squad. Saying that, Adie Moses, Rich Walker and Alex Morris also returned to full fitness to provide even more competition for places.

Justin Cochrane put pen to paper on a new and improved contract to tie him to Crewe Alexandra until 2006. It was just a shame that the deal was completed around the time Cochrane suffered a hamstring strain against Wimbledon. It resulted in him missing the next five weeks of the season.

Cochrane's absence provided Neil Sorvel with another opportunity to stake a claim for a starting place after he had recovered from his ankle problem.

Crewe Alexandra 0 Telford United 1

Mills 2

Crewe Alexandra

1	Clayton Ince
2	David Wright
4	Kenny Lunt
6	Stephen Foster
9	Steve Jones
10	Dean Ashton
14	Ben Rix
15	Luke Varney
16	Anthony Tonkin
26	Michael Higdon
29	Billy Jones

Substitutes

13	Ademole Bankole
17	James Robinson (Varney 28)
28	Gary Roberts
31	Ian Jeffs (Rix 71)
32	Tom Betts

Referee:
Mike Pike (Barrow-in-Furness)

Telford United

1	Chris MacKenzie
2	Matthew Clarke
3	Trevor Challis
5	Neil Howarth
6	Stuart Whitehead
8	Fitzroy Simpson
9	Lee Mills
14	Sam Ricketts
17	Chris Murphy
22	Christian Moore
24	Robert Hulbert

Substitutes

7	Lee Williams
10	John Grant (Murphy 82)
11	Michael Blackwood
12	Richard Lavery
20	Tony Naylor (Moore 69)

MATCH REPORT

The Alex suffered the ultimate humiliation as our hopes of an FA Cup run were ended at the very first hurdle by Nationwide Conference outfit Telford United at Gresty Road.

The defeat was Dario Gradi's first loss to a non-league team in 15 years and came in classic giant-killing style as the visitors netted an early goal and defended bravely as the Alex threw everything at their opponents in a vain attempt to force their way back into the game, and ultimately the FA Cup.

With Justin Cochrane missing his first game since his summer move from Hayes FC in the summer, due to suspension, Ben Rix returned to the Crewe midfield after injury, while youngsters Ian Jeffs and Tom Betts were named on the bench for the first time in their careers in the wake of the ongoing injury crisis.

With expectation of a home win high, most Crewe fans were only just settling in their seats when Telford took the lead through Lee Mills. In the second minute, the former Port Vale and Wolves striker rose highest in the penalty area to head home Fitzroy Simpson's well-delivered corner kick.

For most of the remainder of the game it was Crewe who were on the offensive, but time and time again poor finishing or fine goalkeeping kept Telford's slender lead intact.

Bucks 'keeper Chris MacKenzie made a string of fine saves, most notably from Luke Varney, while Dean Ashton and Steve Jones came closest in the first half to pulling their side level, only to despairingly miss the target by inches.

Varney unfortunately left the pitch with a

Dario's Comments
'Of course it's disappointing but we knew it might happen. They get an early goal and then pack their defence and we found it very hard to score. They were fairly defensive anyway but they scored a good goal.'

Mick Jones's Comments
'I'm absolutely delighted. We had a game plan and we put it into execution and we have beaten a very, very good side.'

The Sun
Hero Lee Mills grabbed a slice of FA Cup history then apologised to humbled Crewe. 'I feel a bit sorry for Crewe because they played a lot of good football and created plenty of chances.'

Tony Naylor in the *Daily Star*
'It's fantastic to come back and get a result. I never wanted to leave in the first place but that was out of my hands. But this is my home, where I started and I've got a hell of a lot to thank the club for.'

dislocated shoulder before the interval, which would keep him out for four months – but in the second period Crewe continued to attack but to no avail.

As time ran out things became increasingly more desperate for Dario Gradi's side and unfortunately, after hitting two long-range shots off target, youngster Michael Higdon was singled out for some abuse from the fans that he really didn't deserve.

In the end Telford, who had former Crewe players John Grant and Tony Naylor in their ranks, held on bravely for a famous cup victory, and were applauded off the pitch by both sets of fans at the final whistle.

Saturday 10 January 2004 – 3pm – Gresty Road – Att: 6,234

Crewe Alexandra 1 Wimbledon 0

S. Jones 62

Crewe Alexandra

1	Clayton Ince
2	David Wright
4	Kenny Lunt
6	Stephen Foster
9	Steve Jones
10	Dean Ashton
14	Ben Rix
16	Anthony Tonkin
19	Justin Cochrane
26	Michael Higdon
29	Billy Jones

Substitutes

7	Neil Sorvel (Cochrane 33)
13	Ademole Bankole
17	James Robinson (Rix 87)
21	Paul Edwards
28	Gary Roberts (Higdon 88)

Referee

Mr B. Curson (Leicester)

Wimbledon

1	Steve Banks
7	Joel McAnuff
8	Wade Small
16	Jamie Mackie
17	Adam Nowland
18	Wayne Gary
20	Mikele Leigertwood
22	Rob Gier
24	Jermaine Darlington
25	Dean Lewington
26	Nigel Reo-Coker

Substitutes

10	Dean Holdsworth (Gray 58)
19	Ben Chorley
23	Alex Tapp (Reo-Coker 45)
27	Michael Gordon (Mackie 71)
30	Lee Worgan

MATCH REPORT

Despite injuries still plaguing Dario Gradi's first-team squad, Crewe Alexandra recorded their first ever victory over Wimbledon to move up to ninth in the First Division table.

But if Dario thought he had problems, then they were put into perspective by those faced by his opposite number Stuart Murdoch, whose plans were left in turmoil before kick-off after the club's administrators ordered him not to play star striker Patrick Agyemang!

With Gillingham having made a bid for the powerful hit man, Wimbledon's administrators ordered Murdoch not to play the 23-year-old, who had scored against Crewe on the opening day of the season, to avoid him getting injured and thus scuppering any possible deal.

Wimbledon still played well though, as they looked to avoid a Crewe backlash following the FA Cup defeat against Telford, with Joel McAnuff, Jamie Mackie and Adam Nowland all trying their luck from long range early on.

Crewe on the other hand were more patient in their build up, and they had to be, as the linesman's flag was raised countless times as Steve Jones tried to beat the offside trap.

Dario's Comments

'It's a good result because we knew that Wimbledon have been playing well and they have athletes all over the team. We've won the game though because we persevered and because we have got real athletes at the back.'

Stuart Murdoch's Comments

'I wasn't very happy but the administrators run the club. To lose men now would be a real body-blow. Patrick is very confused – he didn't want to let us down.'

Daily Star

Joel McAnuff said 'It was just one of those days for us, but it's typical of the way things have been going this season.'

The Sun

Crewe striker Steve Jones punished the Dons in the 61st minute with a headed winner. He said: 'Some people said I was offside but I wasn't. I'm just so quick off the mark!'

Dean Ashton races to retain possession for Crewe against the spirited Dons.

Justin Cochrane broke down with a hamstring strain against Wimbledon.

The loss of Justin Cochrane, who was back in the team following a one-match ban, to a hamstring pull just before half time was a huge blow to the Alex, but midway through the second half the Railwaymen got the all-important goal which won the day.

After being frustrated so many times by the linesman's flag, Steve Jones finally saw a decision go his way in the 62nd minute. While the Wimbledon defenders appealed for an offside decision, the Northern Ireland international stooped to head home Ben Rix's deflected cross to register his 12th goal of the season. Afterwards he honestly admitted his target had only been 10, but his strike proved to be enough to see the Alex collect all three points and virtually condemn the visitors to the drop in only the first week of 2004.

Ipswich Town 6   Crewe Alexandra 4

Miller 3, 9
Kuqi 55, 88
Reuser 72
Counago 74

Ashton 35
McGreal 48 (og)
Richards 66 (og)
Robinson 82

Ipswich Town

1	Kelvin Davis
4	John McGreal
7	Jim Magilton
8	Tommy Miller
9	Pablo Counago
11	Jermaine Wright
12	Richard Naylor
14	Matt Richards
23	Chris Bart-Williams
32	Shefki Kuqi
33	Ian Westlake

Substitutes

5	Drissa Diallo (Bart-Williams 56)
15	George Santos (Magilton 84)
17	Dean Bowditch
18	Andy Marshall
30	Martijn Reuser (Westlake 56)

Referee

Mr D.R. Crick (Worcester Park)

Crewe Alexandra

1	Clayton Ince
2	David Wright
4	Kenny Lunt
6	Stephen Foster
7	Neil Sorvel
9	Steve Jones
10	Dean Ashton
14	Ben Rix
16	Anthony Tonkin
26	Michael Higdon
29	Billy Jones

Substitutes

3	Richard Walker (B. Jones 87)
13	Ademole Bankole
17	James Robinson (Ashton 79)
21	Paul Edwards (Rix 79)
28	Gary Roberts

MATCH REPORT

For the neutrals at Portman Road this game must have felt like a dream come true, but for those supporters in the away end, it was more like a nightmare as the Alex scored four times against the promotion chasers, but still ended up losing by two goals!

At the final whistle Dario Gradi admitted that his goalkeeper Clayton Ince could have done better with all of the Tractor Boys's goals, and in truth it was an awful defensive display and there were definitely none of those 'So Solid Crewe' headlines in the weekend papers.

The most frustrating part of the afternoon was the fact that the Alex came back into the game from 2–0, 3–2 and even 5–3 down, but every single time conceded another soft goal to make the task of retrieving something from the game virtually impossible.

Crewe were on the back foot inside the first five minutes of the game when Tommy Miller scored the first of his two long-range strikes to give the home side the lead. The former Alex target capitalised on a poor clearance from David Wright to drill home a shot from 20 yards and six minutes later he repeated the feat.

On this occasion, the former Hartlepool United midfielder curled home a left-footed screamer after Pablo Counago's lay-off had left Crewe in real trouble at the back.

Dario's players responded well and halved the deficit before half time with a superb goal of their own from Dean Ashton. He fired a terrific volley past Kelvin Davis after an inch-perfect cross by Kenny Lunt to make it 2–1 at the interval.

The Alex then started the second half determined to get back into the game, and promptly did so five minutes into the second period. The on-form Ashton was the creator with a low ball into the box towards Steve

Dario's Comments

'I've never seen anything like it before, it really was an extraordinary game – but you have to say that our defending throughout the game was poor and the goalkeeping was worse.'

Joe Royle's Comments

'I turned around after Shefki Kuqi made it six and said to the supporters behind the dug-out, "will that be enough?"'

Daily Star

Shefki Kuqi boasts football's most dangerous-looking goal celebration. And Ipswich's Finn flier showed it off twice against Crewe – hurling himself horizontally, before dropping spreadeagled to the floor like a skydiver.

Daily Mirror

The scoreline was more Centre Court Wimbledon than Portman Road, Ipswich. With both defences as brittle as England's standing in the tennis world, this 10-goal feast was a delight for the uncommitted.

Dean Ashton celebrates his superb volley in our 6-4 defeat to Ipswich.

Jones, but Ipswich defender John McGreal got there first and turned the ball into his own net to bring the scoreline level.

Crewe were level for just eight minutes as Shefki Kuqi beat Ince to Matt Richards's cross, but again the Railwaymen came back to draw level after Ben Rix's fierce drive was parried by Davis and cannoned into the net via the leg of the unfortunate Richards.

Again, though, Crewe couldn't hold out and the game looked over 15 minutes from time as the hosts struck two quick goals. Martijn Reuser got the first as he spotted Ince off his line and lobbed him from a ridiculous angle and then Counago made the score 5–3 with a direct run at the Alex's defence, which resulted in a shot that squirmed past a shell-shocked Ince.

Still Crewe hung in there as substitute James Robinson scored his first goal for the club with a neat finish, and it could have been all square when Billy Jones went clean through on goal but was denied by the sprawling Davis.

The game was eventually settled two minutes from time by Kuqi. The former Stockport County man beat substitute Richard Walker all ends up and finished coolly past Ince to end an incredible but disappointing afternoon in Suffolk.

Saturday 31 January 2004 – 3pm – Gresty Road – Att: 6,685

Crewe Alexandra 1 Millwall 2

Roberts 65 (og)   Dichio 44, 90

Crewe Alexandra

1	Clayton Ince
2	David Wright
4	Kenny Lunt
6	Stephen Foster
7	Neil Sorvel
9	Steve Jones
14	Ben Rix
16	Anthony Tonkin
21	Paul Edwards
26	Michael Higdon
29	Billy Jones

Substitutes

3	Richard Walker
5	Adie Moses
12	Lee Bell
17	James Robinson (Rix 71)
22	Stuart Tomlinson

Referee
Steve Tanner (South Gloucestershire)

Millwall

33	Andy Marshall
2	Matthew Lawrence
7	Paul Ifil
8	David Livermore
10	Daniele Dichio
12	Darren Ward
14	Andy Roberts
17	Kevin Muscat
22	Kevin Braniff
25	Marvin Elliott
26	Peter Sweeney

Substitutes

3	Robbie Ryan
13	Willy Gueret
16	Aboubacar Fofana (Sweeney 71)
18	John Sutton (Braniff 74)
29	Bob Peeters

MATCH REPORT

Two goals, one at the end of each half, from Millwall's loan striker Danny Dichio, broke Alex hearts as Dario Gradi's side rather harshly slipped to a second successive defeat.

Dichio, who had already faced the Alex while on loan with Derby County earlier in the season and not been particularly effective, hit the killer blow in the final minute with a strike from outside the box, which deflected past Clayton Ince and earned the Lions all three

Anthony Tonkin enjoyed his best spell of the season going into 2004.

Dario's Comments
'I thought we had done enough to get a draw. I didn't think either side looked like winning the game. But we were poor in the first half. You wouldn't believe that that was the same bunch of lads who were training in the dome on Friday.'

Dennis Wise's Comments
'It was an excellent result but not a good performance at all. We were very poor in the second half, but Danny Dichio was excellent again for us and won us the game with a very good goal.'

The Sentinel
A goal at the end of each half by veteran striker Daniele Dichio put a dent in Crewe's home record. Millwall hadn't won at Gresty Road in nine previous visits. That statistic wasn't perhaps as ominous as the Alex's recent form, which had seen them scrape together a generous haul of points from some less than convincing performances.

The Daily Star
Crewe defender David Wright revealed his side's frustration in defeat. He said: 'We didn't turn up in the first half and when we did turn it on we were a bit slack and got caught by their goal.'

Paul Edwards made his full home debut against Millwall.

points just when it seemed as if Crewe would take something from a tight game.

Dario lost in-form front man Dean Ashton for the game and handed Paul Edwards his full home debut in his absence, but in a dour encounter neither side truly hit form and chances were at a premium.

The visitors entered the dressing room area at half time by far the happier of the two sides after Dichio struck his first goal just prior to the break.

The Alex were caught out by a flowing counter-attack which involved Kevin Braniff and the impressive Paul Ifil, who released Dichio behind Crewe's defence. The former Sunderland and Sampdoria player took his shot early, and although Ince got a hand to it, the power of the effort took it into the net to give Dennis Wise's team the lead.

High winds and rainy conditions made flowing football a problem for both sides in the second half, and so it was no surprise when the next goal came from a set piece, as the Alex drew level on 65 minutes.

Kenny Lunt's powerfully struck free kick looked to be covered by Millwall 'keeper Andy Marshall, but on the way towards goal it took a wicked deflection off Andy Roberts before looping into the roof of the net.

The rest of the game was pretty much a non-event as both sides seemed content with a share of the spoils, but when the Alex defence gave Dichio room to turn and shoot in the dying minutes, Crewe were left without a point and heading in the wrong direction in the Division One table.

February Review

Internationals and postponements resulted in Crewe playing just three matches during the month of February. The disruption to the fixture programme saw the Alex lose some of the momentum they had gained going into 2004 and only a single point from the visit to Walsall meant that any talk of a possible play-off place was put firmly on hold.

Narrow defeats at home to Sheffield United and then away at struggling Bradford City had us glancing over our shoulders once again rather than breaking into the dizzy heights of the top 10.

Club physiotherapists Matt Radcliffe and Steve Walker, and fitness coach Andy Franks, were working tirelessly to restore the likes of Adie Moses, David Vaughan, Justin Cochrane and Dave Brammer to full fitness, but they were later joined in the treatment room by Dean Ashton (hamstring), the unfortunate Chris McCready (thigh) and young Gary Roberts (knee) during a troublesome month.

After consulting specialist Dai Rees, centre-forward Allan Smart underwent knee surgery ruling him out for the rest of the campaign. Meanwhile young Roberts, who injured his knee in the Youth Cup tie at Cirencester, avoided an operation – but would not return to competitive action for a number of weeks.

Away from first-team affairs, Steve Holland's talented Youth Team booked their place in the quarter-finals of the prestigious competition with a tense penalty shoot-out victory away at Cirencester Town before memorably defeating Sunderland 2–1 at the Stadium of Light. A last-minute equaliser from Nat Kerr sent the tie into extra time where Kyle Wilson fired us into the last eight with a well-taken penalty.

International call-ups, Sheffield United's involvement in the FA Cup and a frozen pitch for the visit of Stoke City played havoc with our preparations.

Billy Jones helped the England Under-19s to a fine 2–0 win over the Netherlands, while Dean Ashton scored his first goal at Under-21 level against the same opposition at Hull City's KC Stadium.

Dean Ashton scored his first goal for the England Under-21s against Holland.

Craig Hignett returned to Crewe for a second spell in February

Steve Jones was named in Lawrie Sanchez's first-ever Northern Ireland squad – but had to make do with just 13 minutes as a substitute as the Irish were comfortably beaten 4–1 by Norway at Windsor Park. Thanks to Preston North End's David Healy, the Irish finally ended a barren spell of 1,298 minutes without a goal.

Clayton Ince got the glamour tie though, representing Trinidad and Tobago against a Brazilian all-star side including the likes of previous World Cup-winners Bebeto, Romario and Mazinho.

Dario also surprised everyone by bringing Craig Hignett back to Gresty Road on loan from Leicester City. Hignett, 34, was struggling to make an impact at the Walkers Stadium and relished the chance to rejoin the club he left Middlesbrough for back in 1993. 'I'm really excited to be back at Crewe. It feels a bit strange after all this time but I'm pleased to be here,' said Craig on his return. 'I have come here to play some games because I was getting frustrated at Leicester. Hopefully, I can help Crewe get some results to push us back up the league table.'

Dario Gradi was equally pleased to be welcoming back one of the club's greatest ever players: 'One of the reasons I brought him here is because he will fit into our system both on and off the pitch. Our passing game should suit him and hopefully his experience will add expertise and consistency to our play. Craig has always scored goals and he gives us another goal threat because we have been relying too heavily on the form of Dean and Jonah. I lost sleep worrying about either of those players getting injured.'

Hignett may have found it difficult to discover the goalscoring form that saw him become such a huge favourite during his previous spell with us – but his presence certainly helped us through a difficult spell of the season and the manager did not hesitate to tie him up until the end of the campaign. Leicester later released him in the summer following their relegation from the Premier League, but Dario ruled out any chance of a permanent deal because of wages.

Walsall 1

Leitao 27

Crewe Alexandra 1

Foster 85

Walsall

32	Andy Petterson
2	Darren Bazeley
3	Zigor Aranalde
6	Ian Roper
7	Simon Osborn
9	Jorge Leitao
11	Darren Wrack
16	Gary Birch
18	Vinnie Samways
26	Paul Ritchie
28	Gary Wales

Substitutes

5	Matt Carbon
12	Pedro Matias (Leitao 76)
15	Neil Emblen (Wales 89)
17	Mark Wright
21	Kris Taylor

Referee

Mike Thorpe (Suffolk)

Crewe Alexandra

1	Clayton Ince
2	David Wright
4	Kenny Lunt
5	Adie Moses
6	Stephen Foster
7	Neil Sorvel
9	Steve Jones
10	Dean Ashton
14	Ben Rix
16	Anthony Tonkin
29	Billy Jones

Substitutes

12	Lee Bell
17	James Robinson
21	Paul Edwards (Sorvel 73)
22	Stuart Tomlinson
26	Michael Higdon (Rix 89)

MATCH REPORT

A half-time rocket from Dario Gradi certainly did the business at the Bescot Stadium as the Alex produced a stirring second-half display to earn a point against Walsall.

The Alex's first-half performance was nothing more than lacklustre as Crewe's players struggled to string any kind of fluent passing moves together and all too often lost possession cheaply in midfield and wide areas to put increased pressure on the defence.

Dario welcomed both Dean Ashton and Adie Moses into his side following injury and switched Billy Jones into midfield at the expense of youngster Michael Higdon. Walsall meanwhile were without former England star Paul Merson due to 'personal problems' but they still dominated the opening exchanges and deservedly led at the interval.

Portuguese striker Jorge Leitao had already brought two fine saves out of Alex goalkeeper Clayton Ince inside the first few minutes when, midway through the half, he gave the Saddlers the lead.

The 30-year-old got the decisive touch to Simon Osborne's right wing centre to divert the ball past Ince and into the net. No one could argue that the home side deserved their lead.

Crewe reached the break without any further damage being inflicted, and they emerged from the interval looking a completely different side.

The Railwaymen played with a style and passion that had been sadly lacking from the first half and were only kept at bay by Walsall's second-choice 'keeper Andy Petterson.

Time and again the much-travelled stopper produced stunning saves to keep out efforts from Dean Ashton, Steve Jones, Stephen Foster and Billy Jones – a feat even more remarkable considering he had suffered a dislocated finger earlier in the game.

Dario's Comments

'I asked the players at half-time if we were a football team because Walsall were far ahead of us with their passing and movement. The players responded in the right way and we deserved to get the point for our second half performance.'

Colin Lee's Comments

'You have to be prepared to work hard and play with enthusiasm, endeavour and a will to win. Certain players showed glimpses of not doing that in their game.'

The Sun

Foster would have had a hat-trick but for 'keeper Andy Petterson. Despite his heroics, the 'keeper boobed when Foster equalised Jorge Leitao's goal and he ended up in hospital with a career-threatening finger injury incurred in the second half.

Daily Mirror

Scorer Stephen Foster was quick to give his boss the credit after Crewe fought back to almost snatch all three points. 'Dario gave us a real kick up the backside at the break, which we deserved.'

Stephen Foster heads home a dramatic equaliser against the Saddlers'

Petterson's best save was from Billy Jones's deflected effort, which seemed to be looping in until he scrambled back to tip it over, but despite his heroics, it had to go down as a Petterson mistake which finally led to Crewe's equaliser.

With five minutes to go the Saddlers 'keeper charged off his line to try and claim Kenny Lunt's lofted ball, but was easily beaten by Foster's leap, and was left highly embarrassed as the ball bounced into the back of the net to give the Alex a precious draw.

Saturday 21 February 2004 – 3pm – Bradford & Bingley Stadium – Att: 9,935

Bradford City 2   Crewe Alexandra 1

Windass 51
Wallwork 79

Rix 66

Bradford City

35	Nico Vaesen
2	Peter Atherton
3	Paul Heckingbottom
5	David Wetherall
10	Dean Windass
11	Andy Gray
12	Danny Cadamateri
15	Simon Francis
17	Jason Gavin
32	Gareth Farrelly
34	Ronnie Wallwork

Substitutes

8	Michael Branch
9	Nicky Summerbee (Farrelly 74)
16	Lewis Emanuel
18	Ben Muirhead (Gray 80)
40	Clint Davies

Referee

Mr Lee Mason (Lancashire)

Crewe Alexandra

1	Clayton Ince
2	David Wright
4	Kenny Lunt
5	Adie Moses
6	Stephen Foster
7	Neil Sorvel
9	Steve Jones
10	Dean Ashton
16	Anthony Tonkin
19	Justin Cochrane
34	Craig Hignett

Substitutes

11	David Vaughan (Tonkin 58)
14	Ben Rix (Cochrane 45)
21	Paul Edwards (Ashton 80)
22	Stuart Tomlinson
29	Billy Jones

MATCH REPORT

Despite a wonder goal from midfielder Ben Rix there was very little else for the travelling Alex fans to cheer at the Bradford & Bingley Stadium as the Railwaymen put in a poor performance to lose 2–1 against Bryan Robson's strugglers.

Despite the fact that the Bantams were battling at the wrong end of the table, they showed enough quality to deserve their victory with forwards Danny Cadamateri and Dean Windass in particular causing all kinds of problems for Crewe's rearguard.

The game marked the return of an old Crewe favourite as Craig Hignett made his first start in an Alex shirt for over 10 years after

Kenny Lunt holds off the intentions of Danny Cadamateri.

signing on loan from Leicester City, but even he couldn't inspire the visitors to victory against a side who had lost five successive home games prior to the game.

Although they started nervously Bradford were quickly into their stride with Windass testing Ince with an early shot, while the big Trinidadian was also called upon to deny Andy Gray after the former Leeds and Nottingham Forest front man swivelled and shot on goal in the 20th minute.

The game reached the interval goalless and Dario made a switch in midfield by introducing Rix in place of a tiring Justin Cochrane, who was making his return from injury, but the Alex soon found themselves behind.

After 51 minutes Windass, a former target of Dario Gradi in his Aberdeen days, broke the deadlock with more than a helping hand from Ince. Cadamateri crossed from the left of the penalty area and Ince let the ball slip through his fingers and onto the head of the grateful forward.

Crewe then enjoyed their best spell of the game as they searched for an equaliser and duly found themselves on level terms 15 minutes later. Substitute Rix had already tried one long-range shot, which ended up half way to Huddersfield, but when he tried again minutes later, it was a candidate for goal of the season.

The 21-year old midfielder started the move by laying the ball off to Hignett who, in turn, fed David Vaughan on the left wing. His cross into the box was only half cleared by the Bradford defence, and when the ball came to Rix on the edge of the box, his dipping volley ripped into the back of the net past a prostrate Nico Vaesen.

The goal certainly gave the Alex a lift and at that stage it looked as if the Railwaymen could go on to take all three points, until disaster struck with 10 minutes left. Dean Ashton committed a foul on the right-hand edge of the penalty area and Nicky Summerbee whipped the resulting free kick into the box. The ball arrived at Cadamateri's feet and when he smashed it back across goal former Manchester United youngster Ronnie Wallwork got a decisive touch to divert it into the net and ensure all three points stayed in West Yorkshire.

David Wright smuggles the ball out for a corner as Gareth Farrelly looks to capitalise.

Tuesday 24 February 2004 – 7.45pm – Gresty Road – Att: 6,525

Crewe Alexandra 0 Sheffield United 1

Montgomery 85

Crewe Alexandra

1	Clayton Ince
2	David Wright
5	Adie Moses
6	Stephen Foster
7	Neil Sorvel
9	Steve Jones
10	Dean Ashton
11	David Vaughan
16	Anthony Tonkin
19	Justin Cochrane
34	Craig Hignett

Substitutes

4	Kenny Lunt (Sorvel 61)
14	Ben Rix (Cochrane 77)
21	Paul Edwards
22	Stuart Tomlinson
29	Billy Jones (Moses 45)

Referee

Mr Kevin Friend (Leicestershire)

Sheffield United

1	Paddy Kenny
2	Robert Kozluk
4	Nick Montgomery
6	Robert Page
9	Ashley Ward
12	Andy Parkinson
17	Phil Jagielka
18	Michael Tonge
20	Carl Robinson
24	Mike Whitlow
32	Jonathan Forte

Substitutes

7	Paul Shaw (Forte 86)
10	Paul Peschisolido
14	Wayne Allison
16	Peter Ndlovu (Parkinson 80)
23	Colin Cryan

MATCH REPORT

A missed penalty by Dean Ashton and a late winner from Nick Montgomery were the story of this game as Sheffield United ensured the Alex took just one point from the month of February, thus leaving us glancing at the bottom places rather than the top half of the table.

Montgomery's 85th-minute strike kept the Blades' promotion hopes alive despite the fact that they played much of the game with only 10 men following Mike Whitlow's first-half dismissal for a professional foul, and left Crewe rueing

Craig Hignett returned home for the visit of Sheffield United.

Mike Whitlow is shown the red card following his 'professional foul' on Craig Hignett.

Ashton's off target spot kick which flew into the Gresty Road end in the 70th minute.

Dario was without midfielder Kenny Lunt (dead leg) for the game but David Vaughan was back in the starting line up after a lengthy absence while Ashley Ward lined up against his former club as he effectively spearheaded United's attack.

The game suffered a 15-minute delay due to an unfortunate traffic accident on the way to the stadium, but when it did kick off the action came thick and fast.

Ward and Vaughan had early efforts for either side and Whitlow went into the book for a rash tackle on Ashton, before things really started to heat up.

The experienced Whitlow was only to last another 10 minutes or so before he was shown a straight red card for a professional foul on fellow veteran Craig Hignett. The on-loan Leicester City midfielder was clear, following Ashton's flick from a Steve Jones pass, but was hauled to the ground by the former Leeds United and Bolton Wanderers defender leaving the referee with no option other than to brandish a red card.

But if Crewe fans were to think the Blades' numerical disadvantage would turn the game in the home side's favour, then they were very much mistaken as the visitors began to look even more dangerous. Young debutante Jonathan Forte was a real menace to the Alex's defence, causing Anthony Tonkin and Stephen Foster all manner of problems while Andy Parkinson brought a fine save out of Clayton Ince just after the break.

The real turning point though arrived with 20 minutes to go when Phil Jagielka tripped Steve Jones in the area. The visiting players, and manager, protested furiously to the referee, but a penalty was awarded and it provided the Alex with a glorious chance to put themselves firmly in the driving seat. Ashton stepped up confidently, and the home fans were full of expectation, but he smashed the ball over the crossbar and into the horrified home faithful gathered behind Paddy Kenny's goal.

That missed opportunity really knocked the stuffing out of Dario Gradi's side while giving Neil Warnock's men the encouragement to go on and win the game, which is exactly what they did. Ward missed an easy chance to clinch the points 10 minutes from time, but with 85 minutes on the clock, the Blades did get their winner despite some desperate defending from the Railwaymen.

Forte's fierce shot was somehow scrambled off the goal line by a combination of Ince and Billy Jones, but the rebound fell kindly to the supportive Montgomery who stooped to head home what proved to be the winner on the night.

March Review

March soon became the club's most hectic of the campaign with no more than seven difficult matches and a host of transfer activity taking place as that final deadline loomed.

Crewe faced a difficult succession of games with away trips to Derby County, Wigan, Nottingham Forest and West Ham, as well as tough home assignments against West Bromwich Albion, Cardiff and Stoke. Although there are no easy encounters in the First Division, no one could deny that this particular run of fixtures was tougher than most with each club needing the points for different reasons.

Derby and their local neighbours Nottingham Forest were struggling at the wrong end of the table, while Stoke and Cardiff still had an outside chance of the play-offs when we faced them at the Alexandra Stadium. Meanwhile, West Brom, Wigan and West Ham were still very much involved in an enthralling promotion race.

Thankfully, the Alex were able to collect seven points from those fixtures and that went a long way to preserving our First Division status at the end of the season. A spirited defensive display helped us acquire a valuable away point at Derby County before Dean Ashton's first ever league hat-trick upset high-flying Wigan in their own stadium. His last-minute winner gave us our first away win since December and somewhat eased the pressure on us.

That memorable 3–2 victory at Wigan should have been the catalyst for a strong finish to the season, but defeats to

A captain's performance helped preserve a point at Pride Park.

Jason De Vos challenges hat-trick hero Dean Ashton at the JJB stadium.

scoring an own goal on his debut against Cardiff!

With Ince ruled out for much of the season, Ademole Bankole was recalled from a successful loan spell at Barnet to act as cover for Williams rather than having to rely on young Stuart Tomlinson in an emergency.

Fortunately, David Wright's injury was not as severe as first feared and the stand-in skipper would only miss four weeks rather than the projected six. The timely return of defenders Adie Moses and Chris McCready eased our defensive concerns as we approached a crucial time of the season.

To boost our forward line, Michael Symes joined on loan from Everton before the transfer deadline. Outgoing on loan were youngsters Matthew Platt, who joined Chris Lightfoot's Runcorn and Mark Roberts, who extended his stay at Vauxhall Motors until the end of the season.

The club's renowned Academy welcomed 11 new scholars for this coming season with the Manchester-based Nat Kerr and Belfast-born Michael O'Connor already impressing during the successful Youth Cup run. The other nine were Alistair Brown, Lewis Callaghan, John Dillon, Adam Dugdale, Chris Flynn, Tristan Hamilton-Hendricks, Lee Mannion, Anthony Marshall and Shaun Miller.

They will form the basis of the 2004–05 Youth Cup team but they face a hard act to follow after the success of the class of 2003–04. A comfortable 3–0 win over Swindon Town saw them reach the semi-final stage for the first time in the club's history. Goals from Adam Howard, Nicky Maynard and Kyle Wilson set up a two-legged semi-final affair with eventual winners Middlesbrough.

West Brom, West Ham and Cardiff City had us needing results going into the final few games of the season.

A superb 2–0 home win over our biggest rivals Stoke City was certainly one of the highlights of a strange season. The Potters were the in-form team going into the derby game with just one defeat in 16 matches, but as they say current form means nothing when local pride is at stake. A Marcus Hall own goal and a super strike from Kenny Lunt rounded off a fantastic night in front of a full house.

You would have thought that the much-needed derby win would have given us the confidence to get something from a trip to Nottingham Forest, but poor defending saw us 2–0 down within 20 minutes and our mini-revival was over before it had begun.

Our injury crisis worsened before seeing a timely improvement. David Wright limped out of the Wigan game early with a thigh strain before Clayton Ince picked up a similar injury while kicking a ball into touch at West Ham.

Dario Gradi moved quickly to bring Manchester United's promising young goalkeeper Ben Williams in on loan. He would have a profound impact at the club in the absence of Clayton Ince, despite technically

Derby County 0 Crewe Alexandra 0

Derby County

13	Lee Grant
7	Ian Taylor
9	Manuel Manel
10	Michael Johnson
14	Richard Jackson
16	Youl Mawene
17	Paul Boertien
22	Marco Reich
23	Marcus Tudgay
29	Tom Huddlestone
32	Leon Osman

Substitutes

8	Candido Costa (Reich 17)
15	Adam Bolder
18	Izale McLeod (Tudgay 87)
24	Lee Camp
34	Noel Whelan (Manel 60)

Referee
Mr M. Clattenburg (Northemberland)

Crewe Alexandra

1	Clayton Ince
2	David Wright
3	Richard Walker
4	Kenny Lunt
6	Stephen Foster
7	Neil Sorvel
9	Steve Jones
10	Dean Ashton
14	Ben Rix
29	Billy Jones
34	Craig Hignett

Substitutes

16	Anthony Tonkin
17	James Robinson (Hignett 87)
19	Justin Cochrane (Rix 67)
21	Paul Edwards
22	Stuart Tomlinson

MATCH REPORT

The Alex held on for a crucial point at fellow relegation battlers Derby County thanks in no small part to a wonderful performance from goalkeeper Clayton Ince.

Ince almost single-handedly kept Derby at bay in a one sided game that the Rams couldn't believe they hadn't won at the final whistle.

Dario Gradi made four changes to his side, as Richard Walker, Kenny Lunt, Justin Cochrane and Ben Rix all returned to the starting line up, but the Alex never truly got to grips with the game, and Derby dominated from start to finish.

But the home side could find no way past Ince as he frustrated Derby's lively attackers

Clayton Ince was absolutely flawless at Pride Park.

Dario's Comments
'The players can be very pleased with themselves tonight because it was a difficult game and we defended very well and most importantly kept that six-point gap between ourselves and Derby.'

George Burley's Comments
'We needed a bit of luck but their 'keeper was outstanding. Shots were cleared off the line and we hit the bar. The only thing we didn't do was put the ball in the net.'

Daily Mirror
Clayton Ince made Derby wince with a goalkeeping masterclass to edge Crewe closer towards First Division safety. The Trinidad and Tobago international was in top form for the Railwaymen and repelled everything thrown at him.

The Sun
Clayton Ince and poor finishing frustrated Derby's efforts to stay up. 'Keeper Ince sprang to Crewe's rescue with a number of acrobatic saves to leave George Burley's Rams deep in the First Division relegation mire.

time and again after setting the tone in the first 10 minutes with excellent stops from Leon Osman and striker Manel.

Kenny Lunt also headed a Marco Riech effort off the goal line in the opening stages, but it was Ince who would grab all the headlines.

He denied Manel again in the 20th minute with a sprawling save to his right and when the Spaniard's cross deflected off Lunt's chest soon after, he made another superb stop by scrambling to his left to flick the ball away and spare the Alex midfielder's blushes.

Strangely, despite Derby's dominance, Crewe had the ball in the net just before the break, but Stephen Foster's header was mysteriously ruled out by the referee, who spotted a push in the penalty area, but that would have been hard on George Burley's side.

After the break the home side were still on top, but could still find no way to beat the possessed Ince. Marcus Tudgay and Noel Whelan both missed the target when well placed and Dean Ashton scrambled one off the line, but Crewe showed more signs of threatening after the hour mark.

Craig Hignett's header was clawed away by Derby 'keeper Lee Grant and Dean Ashton and Steve Jones both had efforts ruled out for offside by the eagle eyes of the referee's assistant.

But it was all about Derby's attack versus the Alex's heroic defence with Richard Walker and Foster emerging with particular credit. Ince was the star man though and, in the dying seconds, showed why he was everyone's Man-of-the-Match when he somehow got a fingertip to Izale McLeod's drive to turn the ball on to the cross bar and save his side for the umpteenth time.

Billy Jones evades a sliding tackle from Marcus Tudgay.

Saturday 6 March 2004 – 3pm – JJB Stadium – Att: 8,367

Wigan Athletic 2 Crewe Alexandra 3

McCulloch 30, 36   Ashton 20 (pen) 26 (pen) 90

Crewe Alexandra

1	Clayton Ince
2	David Wright
3	Richard Walker
4	Kenny Lunt
6	Stephen Foster
7	Neil Sorvel
9	Steve Jones
10	Dean Ashton
19	Justin Cochrane
29	Billy Jones
34	Craig Hignett

Substitutes

11	David Vaughan
16	Anthony Tonkin (Wright 10)
17	James Robinson
22	Stuart Tomlinson
26	Michael Higdon

Referee

Alan Kaye (Wakefield)

Wigan Athletic

1	John Filan
5	Jason De Vos
6	Ian Breckin
7	Andy Liddell
9	Nathan Ellington
10	Lee McCulloch
14	Alan Mahon
18	Jason Jarrett
19	Nicky Eaden
21	Jimmy Bullard
26	Leighton Baines

Substitutes

2	Paul Mitchell (Jarrett 65)
4	Matt Jackson (Baines 27)
8	Neil Roberts (Ellington 87)
12	Mike Flynn
13	Gary Walsh

MATCH REPORT

Dean Ashton hit the first league hat-trick of his career to give Crewe their first win in six matches. In a topsy-turvy affair, Ashton popped up in the very last minute to dispatch a terrific shot past John Filan to secure a memorable victory against last season's Second Division champions.

Paul Jewell's promotion chasing side only had themselves to blame for this rare home defeat because a lack of discipline in their defence led to two first-half penalties and the dismissal of their captain Jason De Vos for a blatant professional foul.

Ashton won and duly converted the first penalty after being felled by the reckless Ian Breckin before De Vos saw red for hauling back Steve Jones in the area just five minutes later. The Wigan players contested the decision but after consulting with his assistant, referee Alan Kaye brandished the red card to the Canadian international. It certainly made a

Wigan full-back Nicky Eaden is pressurised by Craig Hignett.

Dario's Comments

'I would have settled for a point with 10 minutes left but not with 40 seconds! It was a fantastic strike by Dean. It's great for him to get a hat-trick and he took the goal very well. He is probably the only one in the club who could have scored that type of goal.'

Paul Jewell's Comments

'It's a horrible way to lose but that's life. I couldn't ask for any more from my players. You saw the reaction of them at the end of the game, they were on their knees.'

Daily Star

'I just really, really wanted to take that first penalty and show the other night was a one-off. I know the boss doesn't like the same guy to take a second penalty and when we got the next one, Kenny Lunt was saying the boss had told him to take it. But I wanted that one as well,' said Dean Ashton.

The Times

Defying Dario Gradi, the Crewe Alexandra manager, is not something that many players have got away with over the years. Behind the amicable exterior, Gradi hides a wit and determination that has seen Crewe punch well above their weight for some time.

change for the Latics to be reduced to 10 men following last season's red cards for Rich Walker and Efe Sodje during our top of the table clashes.

Despite Dario Gradi wanting Kenny Lunt to take the second penalty in order to offer some variation, Ashton again took the responsibility and tricked Filan for the second time. The Crewe forward showed great courage to step up again following his costly penalty miss against Sheffield United just 11 days ago and he more than repaid the supporters for that narrow defeat with his wonderful late finale.

Feeling hard done by, the 10 men of Wigan responded quite brilliantly to draw level before the break. Lee McCulloch, only selected because of Jason Roberts's suspension, scored twice to set up an intriguing second half.

The home side enjoyed most of the possession in the second period but both teams had chances to take the lead. The lively McCulloch just missed out on grabbing himself a hat-trick on a couple of occasions and the pace of Ellington was always a worry for the Crewe defence. Winger Andy Liddell wasted their best chance in the closing stages, firing over the bar from a very good position. Craig Hignett should have done better with a close-range header after ghosting onto a flick on from Ashton, while Lunt sliced another effort wide of the target after being fed by Steve Jones.

The Crewe defence held firm and our counter-attacking approach worked a treat with Lunt finding Ashton in stoppage time for his match-winning strike. Without even thinking about having a touch the youngster accurately half volleyed it exactly into the place Filan couldn't reach it and Crewe had a most welcome three points.

The only downside to a fantastic afternoon was a thigh injury to captain David Wright. The full-back limped out of action as early as the 10th minute and would miss the next five matches.

Neil Sorvel and Jimmy Bullard battle for possession during our 3-2 victory.

Saturday 13 March 2004 – 5.35pm – Gresty Road – Att: 8,335

Crewe Alexandra 1 West Bromwich Albion 2

Ashton 63

Johnson 69
Hughes 73

Crewe Alexandra

1	Clayton Ince
3	Richard Walker
4	Kenny Lunt
6	Stephen Foster
7	Neil Sorvel
9	Steve Jones
10	Dean Ashton
11	David Vaughan
19	Justin Cochrane
29	Billy Jones
34	Craig Hignett

Substitutes

16	Anthony Tonkin (Hignett 82)
17	James Robinson (Cochrane 86)
18	Chris McCready
21	Paul Edwards
22	Stuart Tomlinson

Referee

Mike Thorpe (Suffolk)

West Bromwich Albion

1	Russell Hoult
2	Bernt Haas
5	Darren Moore
10	Andy Johnson
11	Mark Kinsella
14	Sean Gregan
15	Rob Hulse
18	Jason Koumas
24	Thomas Gaardsoe
33	Paul Robinson
34	Geoff Horsfield

Substitutes

3	Neil Clement (Koumas 83)
19	Lee Hughes (Hulse 67)
21	Joe Murphy
29	Lloyd Dyer (Kinsella 59)
35	Delroy Facey

MATCH REPORT

All the pre-match hype had centred on the return of Crewe old boy Rob Hulse, but it was old nemesis Lee Hughes who would spring off the bench to grab all the headlines for promotion-chasing Albion.

The Baggies forward was in the right place at the right time to enhance his incredible goalscoring ratio against Crewe and complete a quick-fire comeback in front of the television cameras. During spells with West Brom and Coventry City, Hughes has scored a remarkable 11 goals in 10 games against the Alex.

Crewe's own in-form striker Dean Ashton had smashed Crewe in front in the 63rd minute – only for Andy Johnson and Hughes to cancel out our lead by scoring twice in a manic five-minute spell.

A bright opening should have seen Crewe awarded a fifth-minute penalty when Thomas Gaardsoe tripped Steve Jones after he had cut into the penalty area. Referee Mike Thorpe waved away strong appeals but the Sky cameras only reinforced our belief that it should have been another spot kick to us.

In a fairly open contest both sides had periods of possession and opportunities to take the lead. Steve Jones tested the highly-rated Russell Hoult with an early shot before Ashton headed a Kenny Lunt free kick just wide of the upright.

At the other end, West Brom continued to pile on pressure and forced a number of corners and free kicks. Jason Koumas drilled a dangerous shot just wide of the far post before Hulse and Darren Moore had shots blocked superbly by the outstanding Stephen Foster.

Full-back Bernt Haas headed over a cross from Johnson before Ashton again struck a fierce shot that was tipped around the post by Hoult.

Dario's Comments
'I thought we scored a bit early and I knew there would be a lot of pressure after that and I don't think we coped all that well. The two goals we gave away were sloppy because we got sucked in.'

Gary Megson's Comments
'We were sloppy at first and I thought we got away with the penalty appeal against us. Our defending was awful. Paul Robinson let the lad run behind them and Thomas Gaardsoe didn't get out quick enough.'

The Sentinel
Rob Hulse was upstaged on his return to South Cheshire by a striker with the unhappy knack of finding the back of the net against Crewe. Lee Hughes may be another wealthy footballer genuinely worried about his liberty in the coming year, but he always seems to enjoy the freedom of Gresty Road whenever he arrives here.

The Sun
At the end of an eventful contest, it was West Brom's power and strength, which overcame a spirited Crewe side who produced some delightful football at times.

Craig Hignett congratulates Dean Ashton following his opener against West Brom.

Horsfield with an outstretched leg on 53 minutes and the same player again from a tighter angle just minutes later.

Just when it seemed that the visitors were getting on top, David Vaughan and Justin Cochrane combined to create an opening for Ashton. He took it in his stride before thumping an unstoppable shot past Hoult for his 15th goal of the season.

Five minutes after Deano's opener, Andy Johnson timed his run to perfection to turn in a low cross from substitute Lloyd Dyer and the initiative swung back in favour of the visitors.

The eventual winning goal really could have been avoided with Horsfield simply flicking on a throw-in across the six-yard box to where Hughes had positioned himself to guide home the decisive goal from close range.

Steve Jones did have the perfect opportunity to grab a point with just six minutes left. After being played in by the outstanding Ashton, you would have backed Jonah to score but his well-struck shot went wide of Hoult's far post and the Baggies escaped to go top of the First Division.

As you would expect from a team chasing promotion, West Brom came out extremely positively in the second half with Hulse shooting wide of the target in the opening 60 seconds before Ince made a fantastic double save to deny Johnson and then somehow Geoff Horsfield.

During that early spell, Ince really did keep us in the game with some superb saves. He denied

Dean Ashton shields possession from Darren Moore.

West Ham United 4 Crewe Alexandra 2

Harewood 6, 20
Reo-Coker 35
McAnuff 41

S. Jones 61, 72

Crewe Alexandra

1	Clayton Ince
3	Richard Walker
4	Kenny Lunt
6	Stephen Foster
7	Neil Sorvel
9	Steve Jones
10	Dean Ashton
11	David Vaughan
19	Justin Cochrane
29	Billy Jones
34	Craig Hignett

Substitutes

16	Anthony Tonkin (Hignett 70)
17	James Robinson
18	Chris McCready (B. Jones 70)
21	Paul Edwards
22	Stuart Tomlinson (Ince 86)

Referee

D.R. Crick (Worcester Park)

West Ham United

32	Stephen Bywater
2	Thomas Repka
6	Michael Carrick
7	Christian Dailly
10	Marlon Harewood
16	Kevin Horlock
20	Nigel Reo-Coker
22	Andy Meville
24	John Harley
25	Bobby Zamora
26	Joel McAnuff

Substitutes

19	Adam Nowland
23	Sebastian Carole (McAnuff 87)
29	Brian Deane (Zamora 80)
30	Pavel Srnicek
35	Chris Cohen (Reo-Coker 76)

MATCH REPORT

Alan Pardew's West Ham United ran riot in the first 45 minutes to leave us trailing by four goals to nil at the interval. Former Nottingham Forest striker Marlon Harewood scored twice in the opening 20 minutes before ex-Wimbledon pair Nigel Reo-Coker and Joel McAnuff added two more to pile on the misery at Upton Park.

The first-half torment began as early as the fifth minute when a virtually unmarked Harewood headed home a Michael Carrick corner after a busy Clayton Ince was forced to push a Bobby Zamora shot around the post.

As the home side went in search of extending their lead, Zamora was left frustrated by Ince and even more so by Stephen Foster when he blocked another goal-bound effort. At the other end Foster made a nuisance of himself to head a Kenny Lunt corner over Stephen Bywater's crossbar.

The second goal wasn't all that long in coming. Reo-Coker found Harewood and after holding off the intentions of Foster, the powerful forward turned and fired past Ince for his second of the evening.

Harewood wasted a glorious opportunity for a first-half hat-trick when he headed a McAnuff cross straight at Ince. The luckless Zamora must have thought he had made it 3–0 on the half hour mark after seizing on a mistake by David Vaughan but he screwed his shot wide with just the Crewe 'keeper to beat.

England Under-21 midfielder Reo-Coker made it three after Zamora was left alone to head a cross from John Harley into his path. The Hammers looked dangerous every time they mounted an attack and when the lively McAnuff added a blistering fourth goal just before the break, it really was damage limitation time for Crewe.

It looked like being another long 45

minutes when Ince was forced into early saves to deny McAnuff and Zamora – but by the end of the game it was the West Ham supporters who had been anxious for the final whistle.

The Crewe front two worked extremely hard to give us a lifeline and Steve Jones's well-taken double made the home side surprisingly jittery. His first goal in eight games duly arrived just after the hour mark after he had been put clear by Dean Ashton.

In between Jonah's brace, Zamora should have made absolutely certain of the three points but he somehow missed the target completely after Harewood had surged past our last line of defence. It wasn't long before he had been replaced by Brian Deane.

Jones calmly rounded Bywater for his second goal of the evening and if Dean Ashton had managed to get a better connection to a Billy Jones cross we could have staged a grandstand finish for the 507 travelling Crewe fans.

Our strange night was compounded with a late injury scare to goalkeeper Clayton Ince. The Trinidad and Tobago International suffered a thigh strain while kicking into touch and had to be replaced by young Stuart Tomlinson.

The Academy graduate made his second appearance for the club following his heroics at Oldham last season and he made a couple of decent saves at Upton Park to earmark him as one for the future.

Steve Jones celebrates his second goal of the night at Upton Park.

Crewe Alexandra 0 Cardiff City 1

Williams (og) 70

Crewe Alexandra

35	Ben Williams
4	Kenny Lunt
6	Stephen Foster
7	Neil Sorvel
9	Steve Jones
10	Dean Ashton
11	David Vaughan
16	Anthony Tonkin
18	Chris McCready
19	Justin Cochrane
29	Billy Jones

Substitutes

5	Adie Moses (McCready 85)
21	Paul Edwards (Tonkin 87)
22	Stuart Tomlinson
26	Michael Higdon
34	Craig Hignett (Cochrane 77)

Referee

R. Olivier (Sutton Coldfield)

Cardiff City

13	Marytn Margetson
4	Gareth Whalley
6	Daniel Gabbidon
7	John Robinson
10	Robert Earnshaw
16	Gary Croft
17	James Collins
21	Tony Vidmar
24	Alan Lee
25	Richard Langley
26	Lee Bullock

Substitutes

1	Neil Alexander
3	Chris Barker (Bullock 80)
9	Andy Campbell
14	Jason Bowen
20	Gavin Gordon (Lee 88)

MATCH REPORT

Appalling weather conditions played havoc as Crewe Alexandra endured their third successive defeat. A freakish own goal by our new acquisition Ben Williams gave Cardiff City all three points at a windswept Alexandra Stadium.

The only goal of the game arrived with 20 minutes left and had more than a touch of good fortune attached to it. Williams, who was outstanding on his debut, was extremely unlucky to see Gary Croft's attempted lob strike the post and then his hand before trickling, agonisingly, over the line.

Crewe had been good value for a point in a match that was spoilt by the high winds. Both sides tried to play as much football as possible but it was extremely difficult to turn this encounter into much of a spectacle.

You always sensed that the weather would play a part in separating the two sides and both defences had to guard against the ball holding up in the air or carrying further than anticipated. The wind was so severe that clearances were actually going backwards in the second half!

The deadly Robert Earnshaw acrobatically fired over in the fifth minute after Alan Lee's wind-assisted cross completely deceived Stephen Foster. With the help of the wind, Cardiff were virtually camped in the Crewe half during the first 45 minutes and only some breathtaking saves from Ben Williams kept us in the game.

On loan from Manchester United, the 21-year-old 'keeper won the home fans over immediately with a string of top-class saves. On one occasion he made an astonishing triple save to deny Lee, Earnshaw and then Lee Bullock before Chris McCready was able to clear.

Croft wasted Cardiff's best chance of the

first half when he blasted over from close range following a low cross from Richard Langley – but it was the Alex who enjoyed the better openings.

Marytn Margetson pushed away a fierce drive from Dean Ashton before the Welsh 'keeper was called into action to deny Steve Jones in a one-on-one situation just before the half-hour mark.

When Foster did manage to beat the inspired Margetson his header was cleared off the line by the well-placed Lee.

Ashton poked a 52nd-minute effort past the post after Jones had drawn Margetson from his line before

Neil Sorvel and David Vaughan both went close with decent shots from distance.

Foster headed a Lunt corner just inches wide before Cardiff took the lead with 20 minutes left.

In an attempt to get a deserved point from the match, Crewe continued to press, but they found Margetson in fine form. He denied both Vaughan and Man-of-the-Match McCready late on to preserve Cardiff's slender lead. A share of the spoils would have been a much fairer conclusion considering the awful conditions and the equality between the two sides.

Steve Jones leaves Cardiff City's James Collins in his wake.

Chris McCready returned to the side with a Man-of-the-Match display.

Tuesday 23 March 2004 – 7.45pm – Gresty Road – Att: 10,014

Crewe Alexandra 2   Stoke City 0

Hall (og) 25
Lunt 61

Crewe Alexandra

35	Ben Williams
4	Kenny Lunt
6	Stephen Foster
7	Neil Sorvel
9	Steve Jones
10	Dean Ashton
11	David Vaughan
18	Chris McCready
19	Justin Cochrane
29	Billy Jones
34	Craig Hignett

Substitutes

5	Adie Moses (Hignett 87)
17	James Robinson
22	Stuart Tomlinson
26	Michael Higdon
33	Eamon Zayed

Referee:

Dermot Gallagher (Banbury)

Stoke City

1	Ed de Goey
2	Wayne Thomas
3	Clive Clarke
7	Carl Asaba
10	Ade Akinbiyi
11	Peter Hoekstra
16	Marcus Hall
17	Darel Russell
21	John Halls
32	Gerry Taggart
33	Sebastian Svard

Substitutes

6	Clint Hill
14	Ben Foster
15	Brynjar Gunnarsson (Svard 58)
23	Karl Henry
24	Kris Commons (Hoekstra 45)

MATCH REPORT

Crewe repeated their 1997 derby success with another 2–0 home victory over local rivals Stoke City. A Marcus Hall own goal and a wonder strike from Kenny Lunt ended a barren spell of one win in 10 matches for Crewe while virtually ending the Potters' outside chance of the play-offs.

With all the ingredients needed for a passionate derby encounter both sides had chances in this rearranged encounter.

Craig Hignett had an early opportunity to put Crewe ahead but he fired over the top after being sent clear by Dean Ashton before David Vaughan and then Neil Sorvel both went awfully close with long-range efforts.

In reply, Darel Russell drilled a shot wide of the left-hand post before Carl Asaba shot straight at Ben Williams in an absorbing match not yet 20 minutes old. Just when it appeared that the visitors were beginning to impose themselves on the proceedings, Crewe seized the lead after Lunt's low shot was deflected past the hapless Ed de Goey by his own defender Hall.

Trailing to the single goal, it was no surprise that an in-form Stoke would raise the stakes in the second period and Ben Williams was called in to action to deny Akinbiyi, Carl Asaba and substitute Kris Commons. The visitors then hit the post for the first time when Stephen Foster inadvertently played his clearance onto the legs of Akinbiyi. Thankfully, the deflection hit the outside of the post because Williams would have struggled to reach it.

Hignett then had two glorious opportunities to extend Crewe's advantage, only to be denied by the outstretched leg of Ed de Goey before he only just missed the far corner with an ambitious curling shot.

Lunt finally doubled our advantage just after the hour mark with a terrific shot from 25 yards. Justin Cochrane rolled possession into him on the edge of the Stoke box and after Clive Clarke

Dario's Comments

'I thought the players have worked hard for that, not just tonight but over the last two home games. Tony Pulis said to me midway through the second half "this is going to be your night" and I think I agree with that.'

Tony Pulis's Comments

'The lads are all bitterly disappointed. They almost feel as if they have been mugged because they had a right go and put Crewe under tremendous pressure but it was simply not our night.'

Daily Mirror

Skipper Kenny Lunt steered Crewe close to First Division safety with more than a little help from their neighbours. Lunt put Dario Gradi's men in front with a shot that was going wide until Marcus Hall turned it into his own net. But there was no doubt about his second when he lashed home a glorious 25-yard dipper over keeper Ed de Goey.

The Sun

Kenny Lunt revived Crewe's season with a superb 20-yard volley. And Marcus Hall scored an own-goal to help derail Stoke's play-off bid.

intercepted his intended pass towards Ashton, Lunt smashed home the rebound for his fourth and most memorable goal of the season.

Stoke, who had only lost once in 16 matches coming into this game, huffed and puffed but just couldn't break down our resilient defence. In fact, Lunt created their best opening on the night when his under-hit back pass was latched onto by an alert Akinbiyi!

The former Leicester City forward couldn't honestly believe that his low shot hit the foot of the post for a second time after he had beaten the helpless Williams. You just knew it would be our night after that one!

Gerry Taggart keeps a keen eye on Deano at a corner.

Kenny Lunt celebrates his wonder strike against local rivals Stoke City.

Nottingham Forest 2 Crewe Alexandra 0

King 8, 20

Nottingham Forest

22	Paul Gerrard
2	Matthieu Louis-Jean
5	Michael Dawson
7	Andy Reid
8	Gareth Williams
10	Gareth Taylor
11	Marlon King
16	Chris Doig
18	Paul Evans
23	Wes Morgan
35	Andrew Impey

Substitutes

6	John Thompson (Williams 89)
9	David Johnson (King 66)
12	Barry Roche
14	Eoin Jess
20	Craig Westcarr

Referee

Mr P. Prosser (Gloucstershire)

Crewe Alexandra

35	Ben Williams
4	Kenny Lunt
6	Stephen Foster
7	Neil Sorvel
9	Steve Jones
10	Dean Ashton
11	David Vaughan
18	Chris McCready
19	Justin Cochrane
29	Billy Jones
34	Craig Hignett

Subs

5	Adie Moses (McCready 53)
13	Ademole Bankole
14	Ben Rix
17	James Robinson
36	Michael Symes (Cochrane 81)

MATCH REPORT

Early defensive errors cost the Alex dearly as Marlon King capitalised twice in the opening 20 minutes to earn Nottingham Forest all three points at the City Ground.

Dario blasted his defenders at full time after they made enough errors to lose half a dozen games against Joe Kinnear's battling side, and after gifting King two early strikes there was no way back for the Railwaymen.

The Alex boss named an unchanged side for the game but Crewe quickly found themselves behind when King tricked his way past Stephen Foster in the sixth minute.

It was a quick counter-attack from the home side after the Alex had been on the offensive and winger Andy Reid did the spadework down the left. When his pass found King, the former Gillingham striker brushed past Foster before drilling a low shot which beat Ben Williams at his near post.

Forest debutant 'keeper Paul Gerrard then had to be in sharp form to prevent a Crewe comeback when he stopped a shot from Kenny Lunt and then an acrobatic overhead kick by Dean Ashton, but within 20 minutes King had struck again to virtually end the game as a contest.

The Alex couldn't clear their lines after another sweeping attack from the home side and when Andrew Impey whipped the ball into the penalty area, King towered above the Alex back line to power home a header into Williams's net.

Forest relaxed a little in the second half and gave Crewe a little more possession but Gerrard was in superb form to keep everything that was thrown at him out.

It was a disappointing display from the players and while a rejuvenated Forest under Joe Kinnear looked upward towards safety, it left the Railwaymen staring another relegation dogfight squarely in the face.

Justin Cochrane defends resolutely against the pace of Dave Johnson.

Danger man Andy Reid is tracked by Billy Jones and Neil Sorvel.

April Review

Dario Gradi began the month bemoaning the involvement of our players at international level. The Crewe Alexandra manager was livid that the likes of David Vaughan (Wales), Steve Jones (Northern Ireland) and Dean Ashton (England Under-21's) were all called up for meaningless friendly games at such an important time of the season.

With Crewe being dragged further and further into a relegation dogfight, the last thing we needed was our international players to be travelling across Europe and missing out on a week of preparation at Reaseheath.

Of course, every manager in the land has to cope with this particular problem and everyone at Crewe Alexandra is extremely proud whenever one of our senior or youth players is called up to represent their respective country. It is only difficult to comprehend when our players are required to play in a friendly with such crucial league games coming up.

Thankfully, all three players returned from international duty unscathed and went on to play an important role in securing our First Division status. In fact our treatment room was beginning to clear by the week and by the end of the month Dario Gradi had a virtually full-strength squad to choose from.

The return to fitness of captain Dave Brammer was an added bonus for the club as it was expected he would miss

Ben Williams extended his loan spell with us until the end of the season.

the remainder of the season after undergoing a pelvic operation in Bolton. The club's most influential player returned to the starting line-up for the trip to Watford and played a pivotal role in the remaining six games of the season.

Clayton Ince was also fit to resume training towards the end of the month, but wasn't able to force his way back into the starting line up due to the outstanding form of on-loan goalkeeper Ben Williams. The Manchester United youngster agreed to extend his loan deal until the end of the season, as did Craig Hignett and Michael Symes, who himself

Dario Gradi poses with his PFA Merit Award with Thierry Henry and Scott Parker.

repaid the manager's faith in him with a crucial goal against Coventry City. Amazingly that much-needed 3–1 win over the Sky Blues on Easter Monday was only our third home win of 2004.

Middlesbrough, the eventual winners of the FA Youth Cup, ended Crewe's glorious adventure at the semi-final stage. Crewe lost the home leg 2–0 before going down gallantly 1–0 at the Riverside Stadium in the return.

Their progression into the last four of the prestigious competition was a new club record and the experience will only enhance the prospect of our younger players achieving a career in the game. The football club were immensely proud of their achievements and hopefully we will see a few of them develop into first-team players over the next few years.

The month ended on another high note with Dario Gradi awarded the PFA Special Merit award at their annual award night. The Grosvenor House Hotel in London was the venue for the star-studded evening. Also rewarded for his achievements during the season was Arsenal's Thierry Henry, who became the first player ever to win the Player of the Year award twice in succession. Chelsea's Scott Parker claimed the Young Player of the Year accolade.

Acting PFA Chairman Dean Holdsworth, of Wimbledon, presented Dario with his Merit Award – an honour that has been given to the likes of Sir Bobby Robson, Pelé, Sir Bobby Charlton, Bill Shankly and Sir Stanley Matthews in the past.

'It was a great honour and privilege to be presented with the award. It was a terrific evening and I had a great time with the likes of Barry Fry and Brian Talbot on our table' said Dario. 'Scott Parker really impressed me. He told me about the coaching at Chelsea and asked how Foz, David Wright and Kenny Lunt were getting on after he played alongside them as an England schoolboy.

'I didn't really get the opportunity to speak to Thierry Henry because he was busy being photographed and interviewed, but he handled all the attention extremely well and appeared to be a really intelligent guy as well as an outstanding footballer.'

Saturday 3 April 2004 – 3pm – Gresty Road – Att: 6,749

Crewe Alexandra 0 Rotherham United 0

Crewe Alexandra

35	Ben Williams
2	David Wright
4	Kenny Lunt
5	Adie Moses
6	Stephen Foster
7	Neil Sorvel
10	Dean Ashton
11	David Vaughan
19	Justin Cochrane
29	Billy Jones
34	Craig Hignett

Substitutes

3	Richard Walker
8	Dave Brammer
9	Steve Jones (Hignett 59)
13	Ademole Bankole
36	Michael Symes

Referee

Mr C. Webster (Shotley Bridge)

Rotherham United

1	Mike Pollitt
2	Robbie Stockdale
7	Michael Proctor
9	Martin Butler
10	Paul Warne
17	John Mullin
18	Scott Minto
19	Phil Gilchrist
20	Andy Monkhouse
21	Jody Morris
22	Shaun Barker

Substitutes

6	Julien Baudet
11	Nick Daws
16	Paul Hurst
29	Richard Barker (Proctor 70)
30	Gary Montgomery

MATCH REPORT

Defences certainly ruled the day as the Alex and Rotherham played out a dreary 0–0 draw at Gresty Road.

With both sides desperate to avoid defeat in this end of season relegation battle, chances were at a premium and neither side truly looked like claiming all three points on a rather forgettable afternoon in South Cheshire.

Dario's preparations for the game were badly affected by international call-ups in the preceeding week, and with Steve Jones only arriving back from Estonia with Northern Ireland 24 hours prior to kick off, the manager took the decision to rest his top scorer and play Craig Hignett up front with Dean Ashton.

David Wright returned to the defence after a four-week absence with a thigh injury and, although he didn't get on the pitch, Dave Brammer made a welcome return to the substitutes bench after five months on the sidelines through injury.

The game itself was a non-event from start to finish. Although both sets of players showed plenty of endeavour and work rate, neither possessed the real quality on the day to turn the game in their favour.

David Vaughan looked the most likely for Crewe, while goalkeeper Ben Williams wasn't far away from the Man-of-the-Match honours and distinguished himself with a superb double save in the first half.

Michael Proctor blocked Adie Moses's clearance and the ball broke to Andy Monkhouse, but Williams was brave as he blocked the Millers winger's shot and then showed great athleticism by springing to his feet before turning Proctor's follow up effort away.

Hignett, Kenny Lunt and Neil Sorvel all had long-range efforts for the Alex, which were either off target or comfortably dealt with by visiting goalkeeper Mike Pollitt, but Crewe's best chance over the 90 minutes fell to Justin Cochrane.

Dario's Comments

'It wasn't a great spectacle from two teams at the bottom of the league. We had one or two in the first half who needed to try harder, and that was pointed out to them at half-time, but at least in the second half we didn't look as though we were going to lose.'

Ronnie Moore's Comments

'It was a horrible game but we went for the win because that would've have taken us above Crewe. If one of our forwards can score four or five goals before the end of the season, we'll be all right.'

The Daily Star

Dario Gradi hit out at international friendlies after watching his side grind out a point against Rotherham. The Crewe boss was angry that strikers Dean Ashton and Steve Jones played at half-pace following their midweek call-ups. 'Hopefully we have finished these silly games for the season.'

Daily Express

Arsène Wenger is not the only manager who has the hump with Sir Alex Ferguson. Ronnie Moore's battlers earned a useful point, but Rotherham's boss knows his side would have been celebrating an away win but for Manchester United rookie 'keeper Ben Williams, 21.

The former Hayes man, without a goal to his name since his summer switch to the Alex, thumped a 25-yard volley past Pollitt in the 34th minute, only to see it bounce off the upright and away to safety.

After the break things didn't improve much, although Wright saw Pollitt turn his shot around the upright and Cochrane had one effort blocked in a crowded goalmouth, and the game fizzled out in the last 10 minutes with both sides seemingly content with a share of the spoils.

Kenny Lunt turns sharply to deceive Rotherham winger Andy Monkhouse.

Justin Cochrane tries to get away from Phil Gilchrist.

Watford 2

Hyde 31
Wright 62 (og)

Crewe Alexandra 1

Ashton 61 (pen)

Watford

1	Alec Chamberlain
3	Paul Mayo
6	Sean Dyche
8	Micah Hyde
10	Chris Baird
12	Gavin Mahon
15	Marcus Gayle
18	Heidar Helgusson
21	Scott Fitzgerald
22	Lee Cook
25	Paul Devlin

Substitutes

2	Neal Ardley
4	Paolo Vernazza
7	Bruce Dyer
30	Lenny Pidgeley
35	Hameur Bouazza (Fitzgerald 68)

Referee

Mr Graham Salisbury (Preston)

Crewe Alexandra

35	Ben Williams
2	David Wright
4	Kenny Lunt
5	Adie Moses
6	Stephen Foster
7	Neil Sorvel
8	Dave Brammer
10	Dean Ashton
11	David Vaughan
29	Billy Jones
34	Craig Hignett

Substitutes

9	Steve Jones (Vaughan 39)
13	Ademole Bankole
18	Chris McCready
19	Justin Cochrane (Brammer 85)
36	Michael Symes (Hignett 82)

MATCH REPORT

A huge slice of misfortune dealt the Alex a blow and kept relegation fears in the forefront of everybody's mind as David Wright's own goal proved crucial in a 2–1 defeat at fellow strugglers Watford.

Facing their second 'six pointer' in seven days, the Alex arrived at Vicarage Road boosted by the news that captain Dave Brammer was fit enough to start a game for the first time in five months.

Crewe's inspirational midfielder replaced Justin Cochrane in the only change to the starting line up, while top scorer Steve Jones was again left on the bench with Dario preferring Craig Hignett in attack alongside Dean Ashton.

But with so much at stake both sides started the game tentatively and there was precious little goalmouth action until Watford took the lead just after the half hour mark. The goal was blessed with more than a little fortune, although not nearly as much their winner in the second half, as Micah Hyde's initial shot struck the legs of Adie Moses and rebounded straight back to the Watford midfielder, who made no mistake by driving a left-footed effort past Ben Williams.

Watford then threatened to extend their lead when the lively Heidar Helgusson powered a header over the bar and Marcus Gayle cracked a wicked free kick just over. The Hornet's obvious dominance prompted an immediate change as Dario introduced Steve Jones in place of an out-of-sorts David Vaughan.

The Northern Ireland international's arrival seemed to change the course of the game for the Alex and it was he who won the second-half penalty, which brought Crewe back onto level terms.

In the 61st minute he was clumsily tripped

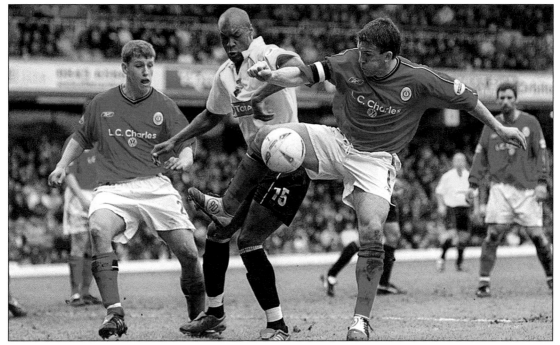

Dave Brammer steals possession from Marcus Gayle on his return from injury.

by Hornets midfielder Lee Cook inside the penalty area and no one in the stadium could argue with the referee's decision to award Crewe a spot kick.

Ashton stepped up confidently to tuck the penalty away past Alec Chamberlain and suddenly the Railwaymen were back in the game. Or so it seemed!

The euphoria of the equaliser lasted less than 60 seconds. Almost immediately from the kick-off Watford's star man Gavin Mahon broke from midfield without a Crewe player within 20 yards. He slipped a pass to Cook on the left-hand edge of the area and although Stephen Foster was first to his low cross, his clearance smashed into the shins of David Wright and harshly flew into the Alex net.

Dario threw Michael Symes into the action late on in an attempt to steal a second leveller, but it was too little too late as the Hornets held on for a valuable victory.

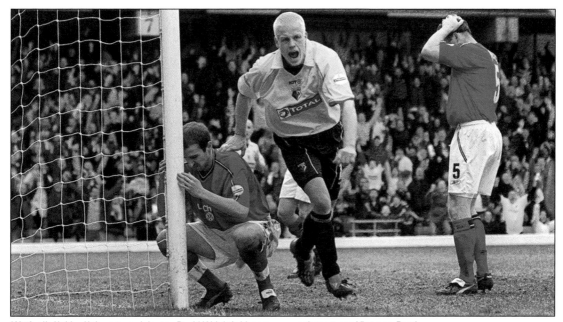

Watford's Heidar Helgusson celebrates David Wright's bizarre own goal at a tense Vicarage Road.

Crewe Alexandra 3 Coventry City 1

Higdon 46
Symes 64
Ashton 90 (pen)

Lowe 83

Crewe Alexandra

35	Ben Williams
2	David Wright
4	Kenny Lunt
5	Adie Moses
6	Stephen Foster
8	Dave Brammer
9	Steve Jones
19	Justin Cochrane
26	Michael Higdon
29	Billy Jones
36	Michael Symes

Substitutes

7	Neil Sorvel
10	Dean Ashton (Symes 86)
13	Ademole Bankole
15	Luke Varney
18	Chris McCready (Billy Jones 80)

Referee

Mr F.G. Stretton (Nottingham)

Coventry City

1	Scott Shearer
2	Andrew Whing
17	Michael Doyle
18	Steve Staunton
19	Gary McSheffrey
20	Calum Davenport
21	Julian Joachim
22	Eric Deloumeaux
26	Stephen Warnock
35	Onandi Lowe
38	Brian Kerr

Substitutes

5	Richard Shaw
11	Graham Barrett (Whing 86)
13	Gavin Ward
30	Sebastian Olszar
31	Bjarni Gudjonsson (Kerr 65)

MATCH REPORT

Dario Gradi took a leaf out of Claudio Ranieri's book and became the 'tinker man' for the day as the Alex stunned Coventry City in the second half to record their first victory over the Sky Blues in nearly 80 years.

With this game arriving just 48 hours after the 2–1 defeat at Watford, Dario opted to make several changes to freshen up his side: this included resting Dean Ashton and Craig Hignett and trying midfielder Michael Higdon and debutant Michael Symes together as a strike partnership.

The move was undoubtedly bold, and in the first half it seemed to have backfired as the visitors dominated possession and Crewe struggled to find a foothold. Despite their dominance, Coventry never really created many gilt-edged opportunities and the Alex defence,

Michael Symes roars with his delight following his first senior goal.

along with goalkeeper Ben Williams, were solid and dealt with everything Eric Black's side (in one of his last matches in charge) had to throw at them.

After reaching the interval goalless, Dario may have been tempted to bring Ashton on from the bench and push Steve Jones into a central attacking role from the wing, but instead he kept faith with his inexperienced strike duo and was instantly rewarded.

Just 30 seconds after the turnaround, Steve Jones broke down the right flank and centred to Higdon, who calmly side footed home his first senior goal for the club to make it 1–0.

Things got even better after the hour mark as Crewe doubled their advantage, this time Symes repaying the manager's faith with a well-taken goal. Kenny Lunt's pass from midfield was inch perfect, and Symes's run was equally well timed, but the on-loan Everton youngster still had plenty to do. As goalkeeper Scott Shearer came off his line Symes

coolly slotted the ball beneath him to double the Alex's lead and highlight another tactical master stroke from the Football League's longest-serving manager.

As ever though there was a nervous period for the home faithful when Onandi Lowe headed home Gary McSheffrey's free kick to make it 2–1 with seven minutes left, but thankfully Crewe still had another goal in them.

In the dying seconds Higdon's clever ball out of defence found Steve Jones, and he destroyed veteran defender Steve Staunton with his pace. Jones charged towards goal to meet Shearer, but as he dribbled around him, was unceremoniously pulled to the ground by the Sky Blues stopper.

Shearer was rather fortunate to stay on the pitch, but that didn't worry substitute Ashton, who stepped up to slot home from the penalty spot and hand the Alex an invaluable three points.

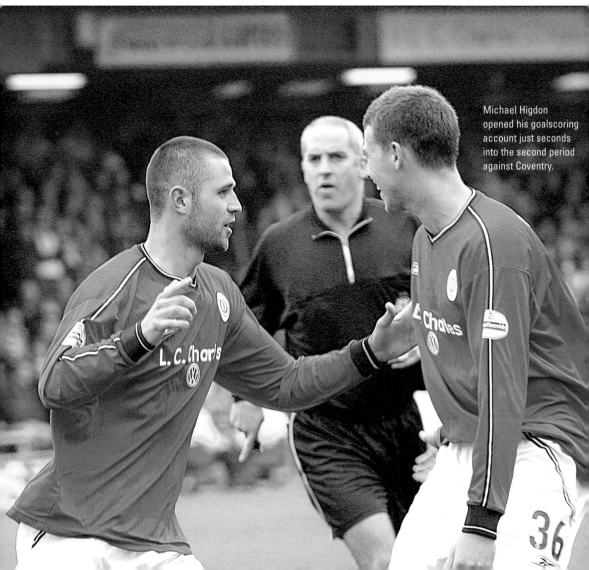

Michael Higdon opened his goalscoring account just seconds into the second period against Coventry.

Reading 1   # Crewe Alexandra 1

Kitson 10   Lunt 39

Reading

21	Jamie Ashdown
2	Graeme Murty
8	Adrian Williams
12	Dave Kitson
14	Steven Sidwell
15	James Harper
16	Ivar Ingimarsson
17	John Salako
24	Paul Brooker
25	Ricky Newman
31	Lloyd Owusu

Substitutes

9	Shaun Goater
10	Nicky Forster (Brooker 77)
20	Bas Savage
23	Dean Morgan (Owusu 67)
26	Jamie Young

Referee

Mr P.S. Danson (Leicester)

Crewe Alexandra

35	Ben Williams
2	David Wright
4	Kenny Lunt
5	Adie Moses
6	Stephen Foster
7	Neil Sorvel
8	Dave Brammer
9	Steve Jones
10	Dean Ashton
11	David Vaughan
18	Chris McCready

Substitutes

3	Richard Walker (McCready 89)
13	Ademole Bankole
26	Michael Higdon
34	Craig Hignett (Brammer 80)
36	Michael Symes (Ashton 85)

MATCH REPORT

A Kenny Lunt free-kick special earned the Alex a share of the spoils as Dario Gradi's side produced an impressive performance against Reading at the Madejski Stadium.

Lunt's 39th-minute curler cancelled out Dave Kitson's early opener for the Royals in a game which either side could have won.

Dario made four changes to his starting line-up for the second match running as Chris McCready, Dean Ashton, David Vaughan and Neil Sorvel all returned with Michael Higdon and Michael Symes stepping down to the bench and Billy Jones and Justin Cochrane missing out altogether.

Having conceded early goals at Watford, Nottingham Forest and West Ham United in recent away trips, the Railwaymen were desperate to avoid a similar situation at the Madejski Stadium, but once again were left stunned after just 10 minutes as the hosts took the lead.

The goal had more than a suspicion of offside about it as Kitson rose to head home John Salako's left-wing cross without a Crewe defender in sight. Kitson, Crewe 'keeper Ben Williams and even referee Paul Danson looked at the linesman for what seemed like an age waiting for an offside flag, but it never came and the goal stood.

Lloyd Owusu was certainly in an offside position, which led to the confusion on the edge of our penalty area. The interpretation of the new offside law is something that needs assessing and Dario Gradi didn't blame his defenders after reviewing the goal on video.

Unlike previous games though, Crewe didn't capitulate after the early blow and took the game to the home side with some excellent passing and movement. Ashton had one effort comfortably saved by 'keeper Jamie Ashdown as the Railwaymen looked for a route back into the game, and they eventually found it six minutes before the break.

Steve Sidwell was guilty of a needless foul on Kenny Lunt just outside the penalty area, and from the resulting free-kick, the Crewe midfielder weaved his magic. Lunt curled a 25-yard effort over the wall and out of the desperate reach of Ashdown to make the scoreline 1–1 and send the away following into raptures.

In the second half Reading looked far more purposeful as they searched for a winner, and Williams, a virtual spectator for the first 45 minutes, was quickly and frequently called into action.

The Manchester United youngster made fine stops from Kitson, Salako and Graeme Murty before spectacularly tipping over a wonderful volley from Royals substitute Dean Morgan. He denied the same player with a block from close range minutes later, and when he was finally beaten by another Kitson header, the effort was ruled out for a foul on Stephen Foster.

It was far from one-way traffic in the second period though and the Alex had several chances of their own to win the game. Steve Jones missed a hat-trick of opportunities to clinch the points, while Ashdown was called upon more than once to save the day for the hosts, but in the end Dario and the players must have been thrilled with a point from one of the play-off hopefuls.

Dario Gradi slightly altered the tactics for our first trip to the Madejski Stadium.

Crewe Alexandra 2   Crystal Palace 3

Ashton 47
Lunt 73

Johnson 30, 36, 56 (pen)

Crewe Alexandra

35	Ben Williams
2	David Wright
4	Kenny Lunt
5	Adie Moses
6	Stephen Foster
7	Neil Sorvel
8	Dave Brammer
9	Steve Jones
10	Dean Ashton
11	David Vaughan
18	Chris McCready

Substitutes

13	Ademole Bankole
19	Justin Cochrane
26	Michael Higdon (Vaughan 71)
29	Billy Jones (McCready 85)
34	Craig Hignett (S. Jones 81)

Referee

Mr K. Hill (Royston)

Crystal Palace

27	Nico Vaesen
3	Danny Granville
4	Danny Butterfield
6	Tony Popovic
8	Andrew Johnson
10	Shaun Derry
11	Neil Shipperley
15	Aki Riihilahti
21	Julian Gray
22	Wayne Routledge
24	Mikele Leigertwood

Substitutes

5	Kit Symons
9	Dougie Freedman (Shipperley 71)
13	Cedric Berthelin
14	Ben Watson
16	Tommy Black (Gray 89)

MATCH REPORT

Defensive errors once again cost the Alex badly as Andy Johnson helped himself to the easiest hat-trick of his career to leave the Railwaymen nervously praying for this bizarre season to end.

Johnson filled his boots as Crewe capitulated against the in-form Eagles in the worst possible fashion after conceding twice in a crazy six-minute spell just after the half hour mark.

Dario kept faith with the side that had secured a credible draw against Reading the previous week, but the solid defending demonstrated at the Madejski Stadium was a distant memory as Johnson's quick fire brace virtually ended the game as a contest by the half-time interval.

After a reasonably solid half hour, Crewe fell behind in 'schoolboy fashion' as Palace caught out the Railwaymen with a standard route one goal. Defender Mikele Leigertwood launched a ball forward from the back and when Adie Moses and Stephen Foster allowed the ball to bounce, Johnson nipped between them before driving a fierce shot past Ben Williams.

Six minutes later and more sloppy defensive work cost the Alex again as Palace made it 2–0. Crewe seemed to have defended a corner reasonably effectively, as the ball was cleared to the edge of the area, but when Danny Granville slid it back into the area, Johnson had been left completely unmarked and he simply guided home his second of the afternoon.

After a half-time rocket from Dario, Crewe were handed an unexpected lifeline after a rare goalkeeping clanger from Nico Vaesen. Dean Ashton's speculative effort from the edge of the box appeared completely harmless, but it bounced in front of the on-loan Birmingham

Dario's Comments

'You would think that we would be able to do much better from a big boot down the middle. But it is not the first time we have wobbled in that area I am afraid. We gave it a go and could have snatched an equaliser but really we have beaten ourselves today.'

Iain Dowie's Comments

'We always knew that Gresty Road was not going to be an easy place to come which made our first half performance all the more pleasing. We showed plenty of heart and soul and that helped to get us through.'

The Sun

Palace hot-shot Andrew Johnson lets his feet do his talking. The in-form striker plundered a hat-trick to take his season's haul to 30 and leave the Eagles poised to swoop on a play-off place.

The Mirror

Crewe were left looking nervously towards a daunting two fixtures against play-off chasing Sunderland and champions elect Norwich City after being accused of 'beating themselves' by boss Dario Gradi. Andrew Johnson's hat-trick took his goal tally to 30 for the season, nudging Crewe back towards the relegation trapdoor.

City goalkeeper and spun over his shoulder and into the net.

Crewe couldn't capitalise on Vaesen's mistake though and within 15 minutes more defensive madness handed the advantage back into the hands of the visitors.

Foster's back pass put Williams under pressure, and when he scuffed his clearance straight to Johnson, the home crowd feared the worst. Foster tried to get back to halt the Palace man's run, but an unwise challenge inside the area resulted in a penalty, and Johnson dusted himself down to thump the spot-kick home.

Crewe enjoyed their best spell of the game in the last 20 minutes or so and made a fight of it when some superb work on the left from captain Dave Brammer resulted in Kenny Lunt stooping to head his cross past Vaesen, but Palace cruised home to seal their 11th away victory of the campaign.

Dean Ashton celebrates the strangest of goals following Nico Vaesen's goalkeeping error.

May Review

Crewe's 'Season of Two Halves' ended with a lap of honour after facing the champions Norwich City.

The fixture list wasn't too kind to Crewe Alexandra as they entered the final furlong. A difficult trip to Sunderland was made doubly tough by the fact that Mick McCarthy's side were in desperate need of the points themselves to grab one of the four play-off spots.

That final away trip of the campaign to the magnificent Stadium of Light was to be followed by a final day finale against the First Division champions Norwich City. Nice and easy then!

Crewe entered the final couple of matches not fully knowing what Division they would be playing in during the following season. Having surpassed the normally secure 50+ points tally, that third relegation spot still lingered because the bottom few clubs made a concerted effort to get themselves out of the mire. Derby County, Nottingham Forest, Rotherham and Watford pulled themselves clear before the final match of the season after obtaining some very timely results.

Crewe's home defeat to an in-form Crystal Palace side had left us glancing nervously over our shoulders as we travelled to Sunderland. A victory there would have guaranteed our safety, as would a defeat for Walsall at Palace. Thankfully, the only goal of the game at

Selhurst Park duly arrived two minutes from time to ease the pressure on the Railwaymen.

As it turned out another point proved enough for us as Gillingham were comfortably beaten 5–2 at home by Coventry City. In the end the Gills would survive by virtue of scoring one more goal than Paul Merson's Walsall. It was that tight.

Dean Ashton's well-taken goal cancelled out Jeff Whitley's opener and the travelling Crewe fans were celebrating on their return journey from Wearside with the home game against Norwich still to spare.

With Norwich also securing the league title before the final Sunday of the season, it was a relaxed and enjoyable atmosphere at the Alexandra Stadium. Norwich, who were outstanding in the first half, won the game 3–1 with the soon-to-depart Iwan Roberts scoring twice.

Craig Hignett's second spell with the club ended with First Division football guaranteed again next season.

Dean Ashton finished the season with another goal (albeit with some assistance from Robert Green) to reach a grand total of 20 goals – a feat that has never been achieved by a Crewe Alexandra centre-forward at this particular level.

At the club's annual awards evening, Ashton collected two awards for his performances over an outstanding campaign. He picked up the leading goalscoring award as well as the club's official Internet award. Billy Jones was also presented with two awards after his enormous contribution in his debut season. His superb volley against Wigan back in December was voted the Goal of the Season and Dario Gradi selected him as the club's Young Player of the Year.

Defender Stephen Foster deservedly claimed the new Players' Player of the Year trophy, while Steve Jones just shaded the voting to claim the Supporters' Award ahead of his strike partner Ashton.

Sadly, the climax to the season saw the retain list published in mid-May. The football club did not offer new contracts to Ademole Bankole, Allan Smart, Eamon Zayed, Adam Yates, Carl Frost, Ian Jeffs, Matt Garner and Tom Betts. Youngsters Adam Howard, Rob Hawthorne, Alex Brown, James Fletcher and Chris White were also released after being deemed not good enough to make the grade.

Sunderland 1

Whitley 25

Crewe Alexandra 1

Ashton 76

Sunderland

1	Mart Poom
3	George McCartney
4	Jason McAteer
5	Gary Breen
8	Jeff Whitley
9	Kevin Kyle
10	Marcus Stewart
11	Tommy Smith
12	John Oster
16	Darren Williams
18	Phil Babb

Substitutes

15	Sean Thornton (Smith 84)
17	Darren Byfield (Stewart 73)
22	Joachim Bjorklund (Breen 77)
24	Carl Robinson
40	Thomas Myhre

Referee:

Michael Ryan (Preston)

Crewe Alexandra

35	Ben Williams
2	David Wright
3	Richard Walker
4	Kenny Lunt
5	Adie Moses
7	Neil Sorvel
8	Dave Brammer
9	Steve Jones
10	Dean Ashton
29	Billy Jones
34	Craig Hignett

Substitutes

1	Clayton Ince
11	David Vaughan (Hignett 77)
15	Luke Varney
18	Chris McCready (Walker 45)
26	Michael Higdon

MATCH REPORT

The Alex entered the penultimate game of the season still nervously looking to secure the points to avoid relegation, but an excellent point at the Stadium of Light and Crystal Palace's late winner against Walsall ensured another season in the First Division for Dario Gradi's side.

With the Railwaymen not mathematically safe the away end at Sunderland's magnificent stadium were understandably nervous going into the game, but Dario was feeling bold as he rested the previously ever-present Stephen Foster from his defence.

After a couple of indifferent displays, Foster was given a well-earned rest and Richard Walker was elevated into the starting line up, while Craig Hignett was also handed a recall on the left of the Crewe midfield and Billy Jones replaced Chris McCready at right back.

The Alex started a little tentatively, mirroring the feeling among the thousands of Railwaymen across the country, and giant Scottish striker Kevin Kyle caused early concern with a couple of long range efforts wide of the target.

One man who was showing no signs of trepidation though was 'keeper Ben Williams, who once again produced a stunning display. He fashioned a stunning save to tip Marcus Stewart's right-foot blast over the bar, but that was just the prelude to a truly breathtaking stop from Kyle midway through the half.

After a long ball had eluded the Crewe defence, Kyle momentarily spotted Williams slightly off the line and hit a perfect-looking lob over his head. The on-loan Manchester United youngster looked certain to be beaten, but instead he somehow scrambled back to his line and flung out a hand before managing to push the ball over the top.

By then though the Alex were already

Dario's Comments

'I thought we were worth a point in the end for our second half performance because we dug in, defended well and looked a lot more dangerous than we did in the first half. We had Ben Williams to thank for keeping us in it in the first half because he made some great saves, with the best one being from Kyle's lob.'

Mick McCarthy's Comments

'I'm not going to knock my players because they worked their socks off against Crewe and created enough chances in the first half to have taken all three points. But we didn't take them and we've conceded a goal which we're disappointed with – Dean Ashton's a good striker and it was a good finish – but I think we made it too easy for them.'

The Guardian

Dean Ashton's equaliser ensured another season in the First Division for Crewe, and Sunderland may well be there too if they do not improve. They have failed to win in their last five games and require another point to be sure of a play-off spot.

Daily Mirror

Crewe, who needed this point for survival, were the latest club to test the resilience of Mick McCarthy's leg-weary troops. And if Steve Jones's 86th minute shot had gone in instead of hitting the post then disaster would have just been around the corner for Sunderland.

trailing to a Jeff Whitley goal scored on 25 minutes. Again the defending was disappointing as Whitley had all the space in the world to collect Kyle's left wing cross inside the area before thumping a shot into the net leaving Williams with no chance.

Sunderland dominated the rest of the half without adding to their lead, but it looked almost certain that they would extend their advantage if things carried on in the same vein after the break.

Things didn't though. The Alex came out for the second period looking a like a different team, even though the only change had been McCready for Walker. Suddenly the Reds looked a genuine goalscoring threat and looked likely to punish the Black Cats on the break.

Perhaps the only surprise was that Crewe's equaliser took so long in coming. 76 minutes had elapsed before Mart Poom was finally picking the ball from the back of his net as Dean Ashton netted his 19th goal of the season. Captain Dave Brammer played a perfect through ball to set Ashton clear, and after breaking the offside trap he kept his shot low to beat the big Estonian goalkeeper.

In the end the Alex were desperately unlucky not to take all three points as Sunderland's offside trap was breached again near the end. This time Steve Jones went clear but although his shot defeated Poom, it smacked the foot of the post and bounced to safety.

Nevertheless this was still a crucial point for the Alex and after the game the loyal away following celebrated First Division survival.

A combination of Williams and Walker deny Kevin Kyle from converting an early chance.

Tenacious in the tackle, Dave Brammer competes with Tommy Smith.

Sunday 9 May 2004 – 1pm- Gresty Road – Att: 9833

Crewe Alexandra 1 Norwich City 3

Ashton 82

Fleming 28
Roberts 31, 88 (pen)

Crewe Alexandra

35	Ben Williams
2	David Wright
4	Kenny Lunt
5	Adie Moses
6	Stephen Foster
7	Neil Sorvel
8	Dave Brammer
9	Steve Jones
10	Dean Ashton
11	David Vaughan
18	Chris McCready

Substitutes

1	Clayton Ince
15	Luke Varney
16	Anthony Tonkin (McCready 83)
26	Michael Higdon
34	Craig Hignett (Sorvel 64)

Referee:

Mr P. Taylor (Cheshunt)

Norwich City

1	Robert Green
3	Adam Drury
4	Malky Mackay
5	Craig Fleming
6	Darren Huckerby
7	Phil Mulryne
8	Gary Holt
9	Iwan Roberts
17	Marc Edworthy
19	Matt Svensson
20	Damien Francis

Substitutes

11	Jim Brennan
12	Paul Crichton
14	Leon McKenzie (Svensson 65)
22	Ian Henderson (Francis 89)
25	Kevin Cooper (Huckerby 64)

MATCH REPORT

With the Alex already safe and Norwich City confirmed as champions the final day of the season at Gresty Road was something of a party atmosphere for both sets of supporters, with the Canaries running out 3-1 winners.

Prior to the game Crewe's players formed a guard of honour as the Norwich players came out on the pitch and they were led by captain for the day Iwan Roberts, who was playing his final match after seven years service at Carrow Road. In the end the game was all about the former Welsh international as he bid farewell to his Norwich career by grabbing a brace.

The visitors were by far the superior side in the first half, playing some wonderful one-touch attacking football, and it was no surprise when they took the lead just before the half-hour mark through Craig Fleming's glancing header.

Within minutes they had doubled their advantage and it was a moment to savour for the travelling support as their departing hero Roberts thumped home an unstoppable shot from just inside the penalty area to make it 2–0.

In the second half though Crewe rallied and came back into the game, although goalkeeper Ben Williams still had to be sharp to save the Railwaymen with a couple more superb saves.

But the deficit was reduced with eight minutes left as Dean Ashton's shot from the edge of the box somehow squirmed away from England goalkeeper Robert Green and trickled into the back of the net.

The Alex's revival was short-lived though, as with two minutes to go Norwich were awarded a penalty. Crewe substitute Anthony Tonkin misjudged a long ball down the Alex left and when Leon McKenzie got in behind him, he tugged him back leaving the referee

Ben Williams scrambles back to make a save from Gary Holt.

little option but to award the spot kick.

With only minutes of his Norwich career remaining, Roberts stepped up to take the kick, but his perfect goodbye seemed to have been spoilt when Williams made an excellent save. Perhaps out of sympathy the referee ordered the penalty to be retaken due to encroachment, and at the second time of asking Roberts slammed the ball home to complete the scoring.

However, despite the defeat, the Crewe fans were once again sporting beyond belief at the end of the match as both sides enjoyed a lap of honour. The Norwich players were giving a rousing round of applause from the Air Products and Gresty Road stands and a friendly pitch invasion after the players left the field saw both sets of supporters freely mingling and exchanging hand shakes, congratulations and scarves.

It was a memorable way to end the Alex's first season back in the First Division and the scenes will live long in the memory of those in both red and yellow shirts.

Norwich full-back Marc Edworthy gets a grip of Jonah's shirt.

Looking Forward

A Supporter's View

He bangs the drum. The atmosphere is lifted at Gresty Road.

Talk about a season of two halves! I don't know how the players and officials felt, but the supporters have gone through every emotion imaginable this season. We are all aware of the highs and lows ranging from the prospect of the play-offs to the real threat of relegation, with a rollercoaster ride in between.

If nothing else, being a Crewe supporter certainly keeps the adrenalin flowing. Towards the end of the season Dario stated that over the last few years we have had to experience the emotions that go with either promotion or relegation. This season we experienced both! At least we can say you get more than your fair share

of excitement when you support the Railwaymen.

Both Dario and the players have recently said that we must look to next season for an improvement, to ensure we are not scrapping to avoid relegation. I couldn't agree more.

Realistically, the prospects for next season look no different to this time last year, but before then, we have the last few weeks of the close season to endure. A lot can still happen in that time.

The younger players have to show that they have worked hard and improved enough to challenge for a first team place. If we are to keep new signings to a minimum, this is essential

The Alex fans join in a 'Mexican Wave' during the Norwich game.

A Crewe fan shows her support with colourful face paint.

The club's young fan base remain glued to the action.

Wearing red and white with pride.

Kenny Lunt, Rich Walker and Neil Sorvel sign autographs before the Rotherham match.

Gone but not forgotten. A West Brom fan shows her affection for Hulsey.

Craig Hignett greets the fans on his return to the South Cheshire.

as I feel we are certain to see some of our top names move on to bigger clubs at some stage. We have to face the fact that Crewe is a selling club and that is the reason why we are always in a strong financial position, which in turn we owe to Dario.

The gap between the top teams in the First Division and the 'also-rans' was shown in our last game of the season with a defeat at the hands of Norwich – probably the best team we have seen at Gresty Road this season and a reminder of what we must to do to reach their standard. Nevertheless, I am sure we will be as optimistic as ever and my good friend Graham Hallett will once again place outrageous bets that we will achieve the impossible next season. The odd thing is, we are now in the position that we thought was impossible 20 years ago. So, a play-off place next season?

Let's look at last season as a consolidation that enables us to move on to greater heights. Next season if we are safe with only half a dozen or so matches to go it will mean we have made an improvement.

I still cling to the words of television pundit, Chris Kamara, who said that he was sure Dario would not accept that First Division safety was as high as he wanted to go. The prospect of fighting for a place in the Premiership, if only via the play-offs, is something he would relish. With a close-season break there is bound to be a lot happening to give us either hope or depression. Crewe Alexandra v Leeds United has a lovely ring to it!

I must take this opportunity to offer the fans' congratulations to Dario on his PFA Merit Award. He continues to guide us to heights we could not have dreamt of prior to his arrival at the club 21 years ago. I am convinced that we would now be extinct if we hadn't had Dario to guide us to where we are today. His continued support by the board of directors has given us a team to be proud of.

Richard Kirkham

Clayton Ince

Dario Gradi favourably compares Clayton Ince with the finest goalkeepers he has ever had the privilege to work with during his long and industrious career. The Trinidad and Tobago international's main attribute is the way he comes and collects crosses to ease the pressure on the back four, best illustrated in his outstanding individual performances against Everton in the FA Cup during 2002 and away at Derby County, Rotherham and Preston North End during the previous campaign.

Anyone who witnessed his display at Pride Park last season would claim that Ince possesses the necessary credentials to become a top-class goalkeeper, but like many of the current Crewe squad he is striving for that level of consistency that would only enhance his reputation further.

Ince's vast improvement in the last couple of seasons has seen him fully established as the number one goalkeeper at the club and as a result Ademole Bankole has moved on this summer to regain first team football. Having joined from Trinidadian outfit Defence Force in 1999 for just £50,000, Ince originally struggled to break into the first team due to the presence of Jason Kearton, Bankole and his commitments to his national side. Slowly but surely he forced his way into the team and has been first choice for the last couple of seasons.

He began last season in startling form keeping out the likes of England internationals Wayne Rooney, Emile Heskey and Michael Owen in pre-season before producing a Man-of-the-Match performance to help the club to a famous 1–0 win over Ipswich Town. Confident at saving penalties, he nearly preserved a point at Burnley in sunny August by saving Robbie Blake's spot kick, but he did secure us a valuable point at Preston by pushing away Graham Alexander's last-minute penalty just after Christmas.

He did endure a dip in form that resulted in him conceding goals he would normally have prevented against the likes of West Brom, Bradford City and Ipswich Town, but he recovered well until a thigh injury sustained at West Ham prematurely ended his season in mid-March. Ironically, that match at Upton Park was his 100th league appearance for the club.

Ten clean sheets from his 39 appearances is a healthy return from his first full season in the First Division and if he can eradicate those odd mistakes he should improve his clean-sheet record this season. A club record he himself holds is of 20 clean sheets during our promotion season of 2002–03.

Like all players, Ince needs the threat of competition and with Bankole's departure, Dario Gradi will be looking to purchase another goalkeeper, who can push our number one even more this season.

The arrival of Ben Williams at the tail end of last season shows that there are a few promising young 'keepers out there ready to challenge for first-team football. That also includes our own Stuart Tomlinson, who replaced the injured Ince at West Ham and may be given another chance to impress in pre-season.

Ince says: 'It was a frustrating end to the season for me but Ben (Williams) came in and did very well. It is good to have someone at the club who can come in and be capable of doing the job if needed. Every player needs to be pushed and have that competition.

'I was pleased to get back into the squad before the end of the season after suffering the injury at West Ham. I knew it was a bad one because it had been niggling me for a while. It took longer than I thought to heal but I was fit towards the end of the season and now I'm looking forward to playing again in the pre-season games.

'I'm focussed on the season coming up and all the players have learned from last season. We are desperate to do even better and want to avoid being dragged back into a relegation battle.

'We lost form after the Christmas period and into the New Year and everyone at the club wants to avoid that happening again.'

Entering the final year of his contract, Ince knows that 2004–05 is such an important season in his Crewe Alexandra career, but past evidence points to the fact that he tends to thrive under pressure.

Favourite Game of the Season
The Liverpool friendly match was my personal favourite game of last season, but in the league then the Derby away game sticks out. I'd had a really bad performance just before that and it was really uplifting to keep a clean sheet.

Worst Game of the Season
The Ipswich away game was my worst game, but I've learned from it a lot. I got up after that and tried to put it behind me, which I think I did with the performance at Derby. It showed me that I did still have the ability and could get on with things.

Best Ground
I don't really have a favourite ground but Ipswich's was a nice ground as well as Sunderland's. The Walkers Stadium was a nice ground as well when we played Leicester in the Cup.

Game Looking Forward to
If you look at the teams who are coming down then they are all big games. Leeds United in particular, but there are some big games and nice grounds coming up this season.

Aspirations for Next Season
We need to learn from what happened in the second half of last season. I will be trying my best to make this season much better as I'm sure all the players will be. The important thing for us is to be more consistent.

Toughest Opponent
There are a lot of good forwards in the First Division but it is always nice to test yourself against top international players and that is what we did when we faced Liverpool and Everton in pre-season.

David Wright

If you are looking for Crewe Alexandra's most consistent performer from last season you wouldn't look much further than David Wright. In the absence of regular captain Dave Brammer, Wright skippered the club he joined as a youngster on 25 occasions and the extra responsibility only enhanced his performances. Odd as it may seem, Wright only turned 24 in May but he has already amassed 240 appearances since breaking into the first team back in August 1997.

Wright's ability and versatility saw him operate all across the back four last season and even in centre-midfield at West Brom when Billy Jones was forced to leave the field with a head wound. As a senior member of the side, Wright, along with Kenny Lunt, suggested the tactical switch and promptly scored with his very first touch at one of his favourite grounds, the Hawthorns!

As a marauding right-back, Wright should have scored more goals than the three he has so far in his career, but his contribution to the Crewe attack improves with every season. More importantly he seems unflappable wherever he plays in the back four and some of the leading forwards in the game have struggled to make an impact when facing him. It is certainly a rare occasion when a winger has the better of Wright over 90 minutes. Dario Gradi usually draws a complete blank when asked that very question.

Held in such high esteem by the coaching staff, it is no surprise that Wright has been earmarked as the most likely to become a Premier League player in the near future. As you would expect from any ambitious youngster, the Warrington-born defender has made no secret of the fact that he would like to play in the top flight as soon as possible, and there are a number of clubs monitoring his situation as he enters the final 12 months of his contract at Crewe.

Leeds United even invited him to spend the day training with them last season and his name was constantly linked with a number of larger clubs in the media after Dario Gradi declared that he is the best equipped of the Crewe youngsters to make the transition into top-class football.

'I'm like any other ambitious player and I want to play as high as I can. I enjoyed the time I spent training at Leeds and working with some top international players. You never know what will happen in this game, and I've just got to keep on playing well for Crewe and maybe a new challenge will come along at some point,' said David last season.

Although the club seem to have ready-made replacements in Chris McCready and the emerging Billy Jones, the loss of one of our most experienced players should not be underestimated. Wright has been a regular in the first team over the last six seasons and his temperament is second to none. He has quite remarkably only received 10 yellow cards during his career and four of those came in the Second Division.

On the one hand, we sincerely hope that Wright can realise his dream of playing in the top flight, but on the other we would like him to stay with us and help Crewe really establish themselves as a First Division club. Either way, David Wright will always be regarded as one of the finest defenders in the club's history. He says: 'I felt we underachieved last season as a team, especially after the start we had. We seemed to do things the other way around because we usually start badly and come good at the end. It is difficult to assess what went wrong after Christmas but no one was pleased with where we finished in the league.

Dave explains: 'I really do think we have enough quality at this club to finish comfortably in mid-table. It is important that our key players stay injury free and that we become mentally stronger after what happened last season.

'We are not a relegation team and have already shown that we can compete with the larger clubs in the First Division. We just have to produce it on a more consistent basis.'

Richard Walker

Following the summer departures of centre defenders Efe Sodje and Dave Walton and the early season injuries to Chris McCready and new signing Adie Moses, Academy graduate Richard Walker was thrust into the first-team picture after previously making just four appearances during our earlier spells in the First Division.

Having originally broken into the side back in November 2000 for the televised encounter away at Preston North End, the Stafford-born no-nonsense defender made just a further three appearances, against Sheffield Wednesday and Wimbledon during his debut season and then away at West Brom in our relegation season.

With squad competition fierce in the Second Division, Walker did exceptionally well to establish himself in the side and was considered a regular alongside Stephen Foster. Walker made 45 appearances during our promotion season and even demonstrated the fact that he could be a threat in the opposing penalty area by notching up a couple of goals against Mansfield Town and the final day draw with Cardiff City.

A near-perfect season was somewhat spoilt by the harsh red card he received at Wigan Athletic in November 2002. Referee Mark Copper later accepted that he was wrong to have shown the Crewe youngster his first red card of his career for nothing more than a block on Tony Dinning. The red card was later rescinded by appeal – but it still cost him his place as Dave Walton returned from injury.

It was evident from his displays in the Second Division and now the First Division, that Walker and his close friend Stephen Foster can read each other's game extremely well, having progressed through the ranks together.

Walker, now 23, was spotted playing for Stafford against Crewe Alexandra by Academy Director Steve Holland and was asked to join the club's Centre of Excellence as an 11-year-old. Having progressed through the Academy (we obtained status in 1998), Walker enhanced his experience by spending time on loan at non-league Halesowen Town and Northwich Victoria. It was a move that paid dividends as Walker developed the need to compete for league points at such a young age.

Fondly known as the 'Doorman' by the club's supporters, Walker made 21 appearances last season – a total that was greatly reduced by an ankle injury over the Christmas and New Year period.

'It is never nice being out of the side and you have to use training and the reserve matches to try and impress the manager and force your way back into his plans. Every footballer wants to be playing the games on a matchday because it is frustrating having to watch because you want to be out there and trying to do well for yourself and the rest of the lads,' explains Rich.

'As a club there was certainly some high points from last season but equally some low points. To be involved in a relegation battle was disappointing, especially when you consider the level of our early season performances.

'We are still a young side though and our inexperience may suggest the reason for our inconsistency. That is the area we have to build up both individually and collectively.'

He began the season in the side and in form, scoring in another televised encounter at Rotherham United and producing a man-of-the-match display to keep Daniel Dichio quiet when he was at Derby County in October. That game showed Walker at his commanding best and must be the benchmark for next season as he tries to force his way back into the manager's first 11.

Walker was recalled into the side that defended so resolutely away at Derby and then Sunderland, but with Dario Gradi electing to go with the more experienced Adie Moses and Foster during the crucial run-in, Walker knows that he has a fight on his hands to re-establish himself in the back four or as one of three centre-backs if the manager elects to play with a wing-back system.

Rich says: 'After playing 40 odd games in our promotion season and being pleased with my performances, last season didn't go as well as I would have liked. That had to do with injuries and dips in my form – but I still think I improved as a player by playing at this level.'

Rich concludes: 'My main aim now is to try and cement myself in the side and become an automatic choice on the team sheet. It is important that we push on now after laying some good foundations last season. The bar has been raised at this club and Dario wants a vast improvement on our league position this coming season.'

Favourite Game of the Season

For me it was Derby away. It was my first game back after a bad run of injuries that had kept me out of the side. We took a battering that night but came through it with a clean sheet and I probably had my best game of the season. It made the work through the injuries worthwhile and was a really special night.

Worst Game of the Season

When we came off at half time against West Ham at Upton Park 4–0 down that was a real low. For me though being injured and out of the side generally and especially coming off injured against Gillingham and missing the Christmas period.

Best Ground

Ipswich is a nice ground and a nice pitch but it still has a traditional feel about it whereas some of the more modern stadiums all feel pretty much the same.

Game Looking Forward to

I'm definitely looking forward to going to Elland Road to play Leeds. I have a lot of family in Leeds who all support them and I was raised as a Leeds fan as well. My allegiances now lie with Crewe but going to Elland Road would be a proud occasion.

Aspirations for Next Season

I just want to cement a regular place in the side and be one of those players who is automatically on the team sheet every week. Dario expects more this year from everyone.

Toughest Opponent Faced

Marlon Harewood at West Ham was a very tough opponent, but equally when he played for Forest against us I didn't fear him too much. But just based on that performance against West Ham he would be the most difficult opponent I have faced.

Kenny Lunt

Kenny Lunt has provided the tactical awareness out on the pitch for the last seven years. His acute reading of match situations and creativity has resulted in him calling most of the shots ever since he broke into the side during our debut season in the First Division. As a prominent member of the first team, Lunt, remarkably still only 24, has made over 300 appearances already and has chipped in with 28 goals in all competitions.

The Runcorn-born midfielder remains very much the team's archetypal playmaker and his expertise at set-plays has resulted in him creating many goals over the years. As the nominated free-kick taker, Lunt curled in three memorable strikes against Ipswich Town, Nottingham Forest and Reading last season to turn those matches back into our favour. It is no coincidence that Lunt tends to stand head and shoulders above anyone else in the assist table at the end of a gruelling campaign. This season he helped create 15 goals for others while also notching up six for himself. His usual abundance of goals and assists only goes to show his importance to the Crewe side.

Away from the specialist free kick, Lunt showed that he could score entirely different types of goals by ghosting into the box to score from close range against Preston at Gresty Road, heading home a Dave Brammer cross against Crystal Palace and scoring that wonderful goal against Stoke City in the 2–0 victory back in late February.

Kenny said in the summer: 'I think on a whole last season I was inconsistent and so was the team. We had a lot of ups and downs and I'm not sure why that was from a personal point of view. The team though were unlucky with injuries and at times we had too many key players missing at an important stage of the season around Christmas time. That certainly didn't help the consistency levels in the side.

'We started off really well though and I think we were all happy with the way we began the season. I think before the season began we would have been happy to just survive, but if we had carried on playing the way we did before the New Year, then who knows where we could have ended up.

As part of his growing repertoire of skills, Lunt's intelligent movement makes it increasingly difficult for the opposition to track him, especially when we operate with the fairly successful 4–3–3 formation. Lunt's best away displays saw him cause havoc at Crystal Palace, Wigan and Reading when he was given the freedom to support Dean Ashton up front.

Considering his overall contribution to the team, it is little wonder that Dario Gradi has tremendous faith in his most creative player. Although not overly physically strong or tenacious in the tackle, Lunt always seems to be thinking two steps ahead in his mind so as to avoid injury or being caught out in possession.

As a former England Youth international teammate of the likes of Wes Brown, Michael Ball and Michael Owen, Lunt is a clever player who continuously makes things happen for Crewe. He has a natural way of communicating tactics and ideas on the pitch and his accurate passing remains his best quality.

Last season saw a rare moment of indiscipline from Lunt, which resulted in his first red card of his career coming in a 2–0 defeat at Gillingham. An uncharacteristic spat with Gillingham's player-manager Andy Hessenthaler saw him ordered off for two bookable offences after he had earlier been cautioned for a foul on David Perpetuini.

Although his goal tally of six is his best return in the rigours of the First Division, Lunt would be the first to admit that he should score more goals than he does. That is the part of his game that he has been working most hard on going into the new season. Hopefully, we will see him reaching nearer double figures this time around, to ease the pressure on the front two, and that 26-year-old league appearance record of Tommy Lowry's is drawing ever closer.

The midfielder added: 'I could have scored more goals than the six I got because I certainly had the chances to score more. But I was pleased with the goals I did score, particularly against Stoke City when we beat them at home. But certainly I am looking to score more next season.

'Several of my goals came from free kicks and I was happy with that and hopefully I will get a few more chances from set pieces next season. We didn't get that many on the edge of the box so hopefully those opportunities will become more frequent.'

Adie Moses

Adie Moses's first year at Crewe Alexandra will have to go down as a frustrating one. Despite seeing flashes of what the solid Yorkshireman is capable of, the Doncaster-born centre back has admitted last season was possibly his worst ever in terms of injury.

A torn hamstring against Burnley in the opening month of the campaign put paid to the months of September, October and November and then, just when he thought his injury problems were behind him, a twisted ankle sustained just three games into his rehabilitation, at West Bromwich Albion, saw him sidelined for a further six weeks. A return in February was then further hampered by a thigh injury and Moses will no doubt be disappointed with less than 20 first-team starts in his debut season in South Cheshire.

'From a personal point of view it has been a frustrating season for me because I've never really missed that many games through injury. I think I missed around eight games in three years at Huddersfield and then I come to Crewe and miss that amount in the first few months of the season,' says Adie.

'Saying that I really enjoyed my first season at Crewe. I've moved into the area for the sake of my career and to have the opportunity of playing First Division football. Now I just want to play as many games as I can after last season.'

Nevertheless, on the occasions Dario Gradi has been able to include the former Barnsley man on his team sheet, the 28-year-old has produced some consistently good performances, which have shown that in this coming season, injuries permitting, he could prove to be an excellent signing for the Railwaymen.

Following the departure of Dave Walton to Derby County in the summer, Dario targeted an experienced central defender as one of his top priorities, and within days Moses had joined the Alex from Huddersfield Town.

He arrived at Crewe in a hassle-free Bosman move from the relegated Terriers with whom he was a star performer in 2002–03 despite their torrid campaign in the Second Division.

It was his performances against the Alex, in a 1–1 draw at the McAlpine Stadium and a narrow 1–0 defeat at Gresty Road, as well as his displays for former club Barnsley in previous years, that had attracted Dario and Assistant Manager Neil Baker to the flame-haired defender in the first place.

After deciding to leave Huddersfield, Moses was available on a free transfer upon the expiry of his contract and the Crewe management team opted to swoop quickly and offer him a two-year deal at the club.

Despite his relatively young age, Adie had already amassed over 200 appearances in his previous stints with the two Yorkshire clubs and was highly rated enough in his younger days to have won international recognition with England at Under-21 level. Perhaps the pinnacle of his career though came in season 1997–98 when Moses mixed it with the best in Barnsley's one-year Premiership adventure.

After guiding the Tykes to promotion the season before, Moses was charged with marshalling some of the world's best strikers. Despite their relegation, the South Yorkshire club won many friends with their dogged performances and Adie was involved in victories at Anfield and Villa Park and, perhaps most famously, a 3–2 home triumph against Manchester United in the FA Cup.

Despite the injury problems he has experienced, Moses seems to be shaping into a fine replacement for the departed Walton and Efe Sodje (who, ironically, joined Huddersfield Town), and if he can bring an end to the niggles that blighted him last term, he could be set to form a solid centre back pairing with defensive colleague Stephen Foster.

Adie revealed in the close season: 'We can take confidence from the fact that we stayed up and we have to build on that with the new season coming up. Dario wants to take the club onto the next level because he has made it known to us that he sick of scrapping around the bottom.

'He wants to see us challenging for a mid-table finish at least rather than have us surviving by the skin of our teeth. It was imperative that we stayed in the First Division and now hopefully we go on and establish ourselves more.'

Favourite Game
Ipswich at home. Important because it was our first win and a good performance against one of the top sides.

Worst Game
Wimbledon away on the opening day of the season. It was far too hot for football that day and I thought I played poorly on my debut.

Best Away Ground
The Stadium of Light.

Fixture Most Looking Forward to
Leeds United away. They're a big club and I'm a Yorkshireman so it will be good to play there.

Aspirations for Next Season
I want to try and stay injury free next season after picking up so many knocks last time around, and I just want to play in as many games as possible.

Toughest Opponent
I thought Marcus Bent was a tricky customer when he played for Ipswich early in the season, although he ended up at Leicester on loan.

Stephen Foster

With only two games to go in Crewe Alexandra's return to the First Division, Stephen Foster was close to becoming the only Alex player to be ever-present throughout the campaign.

The 23-year-old centre back had been the lynch pin in the Alex's back line for the entire campaign, but he missed out on playing every single league and cup fixture when he was rested for the crucial trip to Sunderland on the penultimate weekend of the season. He returned for the final day defeat against champions Norwich City but, although he narrowly missed out on the club's only ever-present record, to be voted 'Players' Player of the Year' was just reward for his efforts during the campaign.

Foster polled almost two thirds of the votes among the Alex playing staff, as his fellow professionals at the club handed him the honour, and although he missed out on the Supporters' award, his name was among the front runners in everyone's Player of the Year voting.

Without much doubt Foz, along with David Wright, was one of the most consistent performers throughout Crewe's return to the Nationwide top flight, and although his centre-back partners came and went, his displays at the heart of the Alex defence made him one of the first names on Dario Gradi's team sheet.

'I was pleased with the start of the season that we had because my aim before last season began was to try and be more consistent than the previous one. I thought my level of consistency, and that of the team, was very good at the beginning of the campaign and we also achieved some excellent results as well,' says Foz.

'From a personal point of view I was delighted to play so many games because last season was my first in which I didn't miss any games through injury. I had one or two little niggly things, but I managed to get through them and as well as the games I only missed a handful of training sessions throughout the season.'

The defender added: 'It would have been nice to have been ever-present throughout the season because that is very difficult to do in this day and age. The game is so fast these days that it is rare, particularly for an outfield player, to do that.'

With Dave Walton and Efe Sodje moving on to pastures new in the summer, the expectancy levels of Foster certainly rose as Dario Gradi admitted he was now his 'first choice centre-back.' Foster though rose to the challenge himself and nailed down a regular place in the first team with some excellent pre-season and early season performances.

He also managed to avoid injuries, which proved to be crucial in the Alex's fight for First Division survival. At times Chris McCready, Adie Moses and Richard Walker were all out on the treatment table together, but Foster was available to at least ease one defence headache for the manager.

This season Foster may have an even more important role at Crewe Alexandra as he quickly heads towards the category labelled 'experienced player'. Despite his tender years, the Warrington-based player is creeping towards 200 appearances for the Railwaymen, and with the likes of Billy Jones and McCready set to be involved in the back line more and more, his experience, which is part of his game he is continually looking to improve, could become invaluable.

His aims for the 2004–05 season are straightforward enough: 'This coming season I want to repeat the amount of games I have played and I am sure my performances will improve with the amount of experience I have gained from last season.'

Foster himself admits there is still some improving on his game to come though. He signed a new contract at the club last summer to commit himself to Gresty Road for the foreseeable future, but if he continues on the road he is currently on, then it would be no surprise to see him move on to bigger things later on in his career.

Favourite Game of the Season
It's one of the home games and I'd go for Nottingham Forest when we beat them 3–1. We went behind but came back strongly to win. I think everybody played well that day and it was a superb team performance.

Worst Game of the Season
Both the West Ham games were very disappointing for me. They were both huge games against a massive club and we didn't play well in either match. We gave the game away early at home and away and it was a huge anti-climax.

Best Ground
Pride Park, Derby County's ground, was very impressive and there was a great atmosphere from the fans. In terms of the playing surface then Ipswich wins hands down. Their pitch is incredible and it always has been.

Game Looking Forward to
The games against Leeds United home and away will be something to look forward to this season. Obviously they're a big club and there should be a great atmosphere at Elland Road.

Aspirations for Next Season
Just to keep improving from a personal point of view, which is something I try to do every season. From a team perspective then we have got to be looking to improve on this season's finish and start looking as though we can push for the top half of the table.

Toughest Opponent
It's a tough one because usually you end up picking someone who you played badly against. But David Connolly is one player who stands out for me. When we played West Ham at home his movement was excellent and he took his chances well. Rob Earnshaw is another dangerous player. He's frustrating to play against because you think you have done well when you're marking him and then he still scores a goal.

Neil Sorvel

Unsung hero Neil Sorvel has been a constant fixture in the Crewe engine room for the last five seasons after rejoining us from Maccesfield Town in the summer of 1999. His tireless endeavour and midfield prompting make Sorvel a vital cog in Dario Gradi's side, although his unseen labour is not always fully appreciated by those on the terraces.

First and foremost a tackler and interceptor, Sorvel provides protection to the back four while his passing links the midfield and attack. Seldom injured during his first four years with us, the midfielder was hampered last season by a troublesome ankle injury that first occurred at home during the summer.

'I was a little unfortunate with injuries last season. I had a couple of niggling problems that took longer than expected to shake off but after the Christmas period I was fully fit and felt okay from then until the end of the season.

'From my point of view though when I look at my injury record over my career, I have to say that I've been rather lucky in that respect,' says Neil.

'When you miss a couple of months of football, you are always a bit tentative when you play the first couple of matches, but hopefully those injury concerns are behind me and I can go on and play as many games as I can next season.'

The arrival of Justin Cochrane from Hayes midway through the summer, coupled with the outstanding form of Ben Rix in pre-season, only increased the competition in the Crewe midfield and delayed Sorvel's return to first-team action even further.

After returning to action in late August, he was named as a substitute for the trip to Burnley and didn't break into the starting line-up until the first week of October after Dave Brammer was ruled out with a pelvic injury. In the captain's absence, Sorvel's experience and dependability played a leading role in seeing us climb up the league table, reaching ninth place going into mid-January.

A reoccurrence of his ankle injury entirely ruled him out in December before he replaced hamstring victim Cochrane during the 1–0 home win over Wimbledon early in the New Year. He then kept his place alongside a fit-again Brammer until the end of the season to take his cumulative appearance tally to 31 matches. During his two spells at the club, the Whiston-born midfield anchorman has now amassed 260 appearances in all competitions.

What is rather surprising is the absence of a goal from a player who has contributed double figures in the previous four seasons. He notched a very commendable six goals in his first season back at Gresty Road and scored three crucial goals against Northampton, Port Vale and Barnsley during our promotion season. He came close on a few occasions last term and has been aiming to improve his goal threat with Assistant Manager Neil Baker at our Reaseheath training complex.

Neil says: 'The two lads up front were well into double figures last season and then you had to go back to Kenny (Lunt) with six. The lads know that we have to chip in with a few more goals next season to take the pressure off the strikers.

'Playing in that central role doesn't allow you much opportunity to get into the box because you are liable to be punished on the break if you over-commit from midfield. Of course, I would like to weigh in with a few goals next season and it is something we have been working on.'

Dave Brammer

Crewe Alexandra were cruelly deprived of the services of revered captain Dave Brammer for much of last season. A pelvic injury sustained in the 3–0 away defeat at Cardiff City in late September ruled him out of the next three games before he suffered a reoccurrence at home to Derby County in his first comeback. Unfortunately, Brammer was forced to leave the field in the 44th minute after playing a pivotal role in a memorable 3–0 victory.

He wouldn't return to first-team action until the Easter weekend visit to Watford but his inclusion in the last remaining six games of the campaign helped the club secure enough points to avoid the drop for the second time in three seasons. Crewe had been crying out for an on-the-pitch leader for much of the season and Brammer's timely return was a huge boost to manager Dario Gradi and the rest of the squad.

Dave revealed over the summer: 'It has obviously been quite a frustrating season for me personally because I spent so long out with injury. Things started badly at Wimbledon on the opening day because that was a very disappointing result after going a goal up and I didn't think we did ourselves justice that day. The game was an anti-climax after the hard work we had put in during the summer.

'Things certainly got better after that with the results we had over Ipswich, Sunderland and Nottingham Forest. We played really well at home and should have got wins at places like Millwall.

He added: 'Then I got injured and that was a terrible time for me personally. I came back against Derby and then had a set back and it just seemed that I would never get back playing again. At the time you wonder if you will ever play but I had to stay positive not just for me, but also for my family.'

Crewe certainly missed his leadership and experience out on the pitch, especially when we entered a bad patch in the New Year. The motivational captain always makes a positive impact when he is on the pitch and his words of wisdom certainly help the others around him. It is no wonder; Dario regards him as the most inspirational player he has worked with at Crewe during his 21-year-old career.

Even when things are not going according to plan, Brammer's appetite for possession never diminishes and he is constantly seeking to find space to receive a pass from a teammate. His all-action midfield performances virtually guarantee him a starting berth when he is fit, but frustratingly for Dave and the supporters he has only recently became a club centurion.

A succession of injuries have combined to stall his progress as a Crewe player and many still believe that the groin injury he sustained in our FA Cup meeting with Everton cost us our First Division status in 2002, he has been that indispensable during the last three seasons.

As the club's costliest player, Brammer signed from neighbouring Port Vale at the height of the television injection of cash from ITV Digital's doomed coverage of the Football League. Brammer completed a £500,000 move during the summer of 2001 and quickly established himself in the hub of the midfield. He made 36 appearances before injury cut short his first season in late February, but he returned for the start of our promotion season in which he played 49 of our 52 games.

Brammer has shown tremendous strength of character to overcome the loss of five months of football and his supreme authority around the club has made him immensely popular with everyone connected with the club. Therefore, he will be a difficult player to replace if he and the club cannot agree on a new contract before the start of the new season. One thing is for sure; the club will be doing their level best to extend Dave Brammer's time with us.

'It was great to play again when we went to Watford, although I was tired towards the end of the match, and I was pleased that I had no further problems during the run in and was able to get some games under my belt,' says Dave.

'In all honesty the season ended too early for me really and if I could have bought another 10 games then I would have done. It was a good achievement for us to survive this season after only just coming up, but we are a little disappointed we didn't finish higher up the table after the start we made.'

Steve Jones

Steve Jones must look back over the last couple of years and seriously pinch himself when he recalls how quickly and well things have gone for him since signing from Leigh RMI in the summer of 2001. Having scored 21 goals for Leigh in his final season, Crewe had to fend off interest from other clubs in securing his signature for a fee of £75,000. He has proved to be a real bargain over the last couple of seasons, but things didn't run that smoothly for him after his arrival in South Cheshire.

His tentative full debut away at Sheffield United in October 2001 suggested that the former Sligo Rovers and Blackpool front man wasn't anywhere near making the step up to First Division football. He was soon loaned out to Rochdale, where he scored once against Scunthorpe in six starts.

It is never nice being relegated, but on the positive side a year in the Second Division did Steve Jones no harm at all. Battling it out for a starting place with Hulse, Jack and Ashton, the Londonderry-born Jones had to wait patiently for a real chance to shine. He began the season as an often-used second-half substitute until he was finally given the nod for the visit of Queens Park Rangers on 5 October 2002. It is no exaggeration to suggest that his two winning goals that day transformed his Crewe career.

From that game on, he oozed the confidence to take on any defence in the Division and proved that he could fill the void vacated by the fans' favourite Rodney Jack. Blessed with incredible pace and skill, Jones tormented the Second Division, scoring 11 times in his 38 appearances. His sparkling club form resulted in him receiving an international call-up for Northern Ireland and he finished the campaign by representing his beloved country against the likes of Italy and Spain!

With his apprenticeship well and truly served, Jones now had the chance to show what he could really do at First Division level. With Jack and Hulse gone, the responsibility placed on his and Ashton's shoulders cannot be underestimated. The question on everyone's lips was could the partnership reproduce their form in the First Division and would we score enough goals to survive? They answered those doubts in emphatic fashion. The partnership produced 36 goals and had Crewe flirting with the top half of the table until the turn of the year.

Jonah admits: 'This was my first full season in the First Division, so I was pleased with my contribution because the last time I played in this league when I first signed for the club I didn't do very well.

'I was pleased with my goal tally though because I certainly didn't expect to get as many as I did at the beginning of the season, although I didn't set myself any specific targets. Having said that I still should have scored more goals last season because I had plenty more opportunities to score. I also got brought down for penalties a few times when I was clean through.

'I thought the first half of last season, on a personal level, was really good, but I think I let myself down a little bit in the second half. I don't really know why that was but I did have one or two injuries, which I carried but couldn't shake off, and maybe there was a little bit of bad luck involved as well.'

Having worked hard on his physical attributes, Jones showed everyone that he could cope with the demands of First Division football and both he and Ashton showed their commitment to the cause by playing when not truly 100 percent fit.

Jones established himself as the perfect foil for his strike partner Ashton and his direct counter-attacking play made him a key asset in our first season back in the First Division. He became a maker as well as a well as a taker of goals. Impressively Jones created six goals for others during the season and was more often than not brought down for penalties!

'The strike partnership with Dean (Ashton) has gone really well and I think I am right in saying that it was one of the most productive in the First Division in terms of goals. We seemed to click immediately and that was especially pleasing, as I had never really played up front with Dean before. In the past I had partnered Rob Hulse, or Rodney Jack and myself have been wide of the big striker,' says Steve.

'It would have been nice to finish as top scorer but that isn't something that really bothers me too much. In fact I was delighted for Dean to get that honour because he is the more recognised striker in the team.'

Jones, who is now just 27 goals short of 100 career goals, played a leading role for Crewe Alexandra last season and much will be expected of him again this time around. When he is firing on all cylinders he is virtually unstoppable and that is why he has become a regular fixture in the Northern Ireland squad over the last couple of seasons.

Next up on that remarkable adventure could see him facing Wales and England in World Cup qualifying matches. His progression from the non-league scene to international football has been nothing short of extraordinary, but well deserved.

Best Game
Sunderland at home. I thought we played really well and it was fantastic for me as I scored two goals.

Worst Game
Ipswich away. We got hammered that day conceding six goals and every time we got back in the game we conceded again.

Best Away Ground
The Stadium of Light is a magnificent ground.

Fixture Looking Forward to
It has to be Leeds United away.

Aspirations for Next Season
Just to finish as high in the league table as we possibly can. On a personal level I would like to score more goals and push towards the 20 mark.

Toughest Opponent
Graeme Murty of Reading. He was their right-back but he kept bombing forward all the time so I was chasing up and down the wing all afternoon.

Dean Ashton

Dario Gradi admitted he lost more sleep worrying about the fitness levels of Dean Ashton than anything else last season. Ashton, born in Wiltshire but raised in neighbouring Holmes Chapel, scored a cumulative tally of 20 goals to enhance his own growing reputation and help Crewe Alexandra avoid the fear of relegation. Without him we would most certainly have struggled to survive.

It was a huge year for Ashton following the departure of the club's previous top marksman Rob Hulse and he accepted the entrusted responsibility with confidence and purpose. He was goal-hungry throughout the season and received his just rewards by being placed alongside the likes of Marlon Harewood, Andy Johnson, Robert Earnshaw and Nathan Ellington in the First Division goalscoring charts.

His outstanding form also saw him called up to David Platt's England Under-21 side for the first time, scoring on his full debut against Holland at Hull City's KC Stadium and then again in Sweden. Technically accomplished both on the ground and in the air, Ashton masterminded Crewe's survival bid more than anybody else by scoring his first league hat-trick at Wigan Athletic and scoring the priceless equaliser against Sunderland, which guaranteed us football at this level.

Last season saw Ashton fully realise his potential and become a cornerstone of Dario Gradi's young side. Widely considered as one of the best young players outside of the Premier League, Ashton's ruthless streak in front of goal made him (fitness permitting) a certain starter in Dario's side and thankfully he remained relatively injury free throughout the campaign. He was involved in 47 of our 49 matches and surpassed the 50-goal mark with a finely taken penalty at Watford back in April.

Dean was understandably pleased with his own goal return: 'Last season I was very pleased that I managed to beat my scoring record from the previous year. In the Second Division I scored 16 in all competitions so it was good to beat that last year.

'Obviously it was also extremely pleasing to have played so many games as I have this season. I haven't played that many times in a single season before so it is a positive step forwards for me. I also stayed clear of any major injury problems as well.

He added: 'Perhaps the best thing though was the fact that I was more consistent throughout the matches that I played. I think I really struggled for consistency in the Second Division and last season was much better, even though I still aim to improve that side of my game.'

Of course, Ashton broke into the first team as a 16-year-old nearly four years ago after scoring goals for fun at Academy and Youth Team level. His eight goals in just 13 starts during that debut season inevitably propelled him into the public arena. To his credit, he handled the rave reviews and big headlines with relative ease and it was only niggling injuries that hampered his progress.

A steady flow of goals continued with him scoring 26 in the last two seasons, before his exceptional 20 during the last campaign. The opportunistic striker is never afraid to shoot and he scored some stylish goals last season. His swivel and shot against Burnley, his headed goals against Sunderland and Nottingham Forest and the powerful drive against West Brom were goals only bettered by his terrific winner at the JJB Stadium. It is no exaggeration to suggest that only Ashton had the ability to covert that half chance. That type of form saw him earn a place in David Platt's England Under-21 side:

'On the international front the England Under-21 call up was another positive and I was very happy to play, and then score, on my debut against Holland last season. It was very pleasing although now that David Platt is no longer the manager I will have to wait and see what happens,' says Dean.

Ashton has worked hard on the club's weights programme and his powerful frame makes him a handful for any defence. He is usually the first to arrive at training at Reaseheath and is more often than not the last to leave. That hard work has most certainly paid off and the Crewe number 10 should go from strength to strength during this coming season.

Dean admitted in pre-season: 'I think overall we were a little disappointed with the way we finished last season, but looking back on the way we played at the beginning and in the middle of the season then that is something positive that we can take into the new season.'

Best Game
Wigan away where I scored a hat-trick.

Worst Game
Watford at home where we lost 1–0 against 10 men.

Best Away Ground
Derby County's Pride Park.

Fixture looking forward to
Wolves away. Molineux is a tremendous stadium.

Aspirations for next season
I'm hoping that we can finish a lot higher in the table and I need to improve my consistency and also score more goals.

Toughest Opponent
Tomas Repka of West Ham. He was horrible to play against.

David Vaughan

Crewe Alexandra's Welsh international David Vaughan is finally beginning to establish himself in Dario Gradi's starting 11 as well as Mark Hughes's international squad. The technically accomplished youngster was the first to breakthrough from that relatively successful group of 12 who were signed in January 2001.

He actually made his first-team debut some five months before signing professional forms with the club, but only lasted 45 minutes against Blackburn Rovers in our first home game of that particular season. Maybe that chance came a little too early for the Rhuddlan-born midfielder, but it was only a matter of time before Vaughan was challenging for a leading role in the side. His full league debut duly arrived on Boxing Day 2001 at Walsall's Bescot Stadium.

Vaughan may not be the quickest thing on two legs but his mind is always brimming with invention and there are few better passers at the club than the natural left-footer. He is forever looking to open up the opposition defence with a deft through ball or foray down the flank into enemy territory and swinging those dangerous crosses into the danger zone. He can often be our secret weapon going forward as his four goal assists from last season clearly demonstrate.

His accurate crosses created goals for Stephen Foster and Kenny Lunt against Preston at the Alexandra Stadium and even that was bettered by his sublime cross for Dean Ashton to head home a leveller against Nottingham Forest back in September. Dario Gradi does not hide the fact that he wants more of that match-winning ability from his talented winger.

Unsurprisingly, he also requires more goals from a player who used to score so regularly in the Academy. Vaughan failed to score at all last season in his 33 appearances and has strangely only found the net on five occasions during his career so far.

Of course, Vaughan has been asked to fill in at left-back on numerous occasions over the last three seasons and his adventurous interpretation of that defensive role has clearly found favour with Dario and many supporters. Observers tend to argue that Vaughan is more dangerous going forward from a deeper position as he has more space to exploit with his excellent close control. Maybe the wing-back role would suit his attributes the most?

Vaughan diplomatically states: I'm not sure what position I prefer. Looking back at last season most of my better games have come playing at left-back but you do tend to get more involved in the game playing in midfield. For me though that is a harder position to play, but when I am playing well I do like playing wide on the left.

'Things seemed to be going really well before I got injured at Norwich but after I came back it took me a while to get back to my best. I think I improved for the last few games of the season and was on something like my best form again.'

Vaughan's creative instincts have not gone unnoticed at international level either, and he has been a part of the Welsh set-up for the last two years. He scored his first Under-21 goal with a quick free kick in Italy in September, while progressing to the senior squad for friendly encounters in the United States and Hungary.

'It's great that I have managed to force my way into Mark Hughes's squad, which is something I didn't really expect. I think myself and one other lad are the youngest in the team at the moment and it is really helping my game to be involved at international level,' says David.

Like many of the younger players in the Crewe squad, Dario Gradi will be looking for more consistent displays from a player who is never afraid to dig in and fight when necessary. Vaughan has many strings to his bow and that is why the club were so determined to bind him to the club until 2007 in the latest rounds of contract negotiations.

Favourite Game of the Season
Well the best game this season has to be when we defeated Stoke City at Gresty Road in March. It was a big three points for us and obviously that was added to the fact that it was a local derby.

Worst Game of the Season
Definitely the worst game I can remember is the home defeat at the hands of Watford back in October. They were down to 10 men, but we played poorly throughout that game and it was summed up at the end when they scored a late winner.

Best Ground
The Stadium of Light is my favourite ground where we secured our First Division status.

Game Looking Forward to
Like most people I am looking forward to playing at the grounds of the big clubs. Obviously Leeds United at Elland Road springs to mind straight away.

Aspirations for Next Season
We have got to be looking to finish a lot higher up the table than we did last season. I think realistically we need to be setting our sights on the top half after the way we started last season.

Toughest Opponent
Jobi McAnuff of West Ham and previously with Wimbledon. I played against him at West Ham and he was lightening quick, his pace was incredible and it was a tough job to stay with him.

Ben Rix

The pre-season performances of Ben Rix suggested that the 2003–04 season would finally see the Wolverhampton-born youngster realise his vast potential. He was comfortably our most effective player during the pre-season friendly encounters against the likes of Liverpool, Everton, Tranmere and Port Vale and he quite deservedly kept his place for the opening 10 matches of the season.

Well-taken goals in the summer against Everton and Port Vale showed that Rix has the necessary ability to add goals to his all round game. His previous goals at senior level, ironically both coming in the early minutes of FA Cup ties against Sheffield Wednesday and Mansfield Town, also indicate that he has the legs to make late, untracked runs into the opposing penalty area before applying a composed finish. That was later supported by his first-ever league goal against Derby County in October, when after coming on as a substitute for Andrew Barrowman he raced onto a Kenny Lunt through ball before clipping it perfectly over Lee Grant's head to round off a fine 3–0 victory.

Niggling injuries stalled his early season form and Rix struggled to re-establish himself in Dario Gradi's starting 11 after that setback – but he was more often than not named on the substitutes bench until he suffered a broken toe away at Gillingham in early December. That ruled him out for a further month until he was able to return for the FA Cup tie with Telford United.

Ben admits: 'The injuries were frustrating. I missed the Cardiff game away and then I broke my toe against Gillingham, which put me out for about a month. That was irritating because the year before I did all my ligaments in my ankle and that kept me out for eight weeks, but hopefully this year I will be injury free.

'The first half of last season was quite a success for me but the second half of the season wasn't so good. I fell out of form a bit and it was certainly disappointing to finish the season in the way that I did.

'The most important thing though was the team, and although I don't think last season was an excellent season because we wanted to finish a lot higher up the table, to stay up was the main aim at the start of the season. If you had told us that we would finish where we did and stayed up safely at the beginning of last season then we would have all said fair enough.'

In-and-out for much of the season, it was a frustrating time for one of the club's brightest young midfield players, with the only other highlight his wonderfully struck goal away at Bradford City after he had replaced Justin Cochrane at the half-time interval. An individual with outstanding technical merit, it was a goal that only underlined his growing reputation.

'I don't really know what went wrong for me in the second half of the season. To be honest the position I play is really hard to play week in and week out and there are lots of good players vying for that place,' says a frustrated Ben.

'Vaughany is probably a better winger than me anyway, and so it is hard to keep a place down. Then, when you are not playing week in and week out it can be hard to come back into the team and do well straight away.'

Make no mistake about it, Rix will be using the summer 'break' to toughen himself up with intense activity at the training ground to make sure he is in prime condition to make a significant mark in this forthcoming season. He is keen to play more of a starting role in the side and was disappointed to have been a peripheral figure in the club's sixth season at this level. Rix has a fight on his hands to break into a highly competitive midfield, but he is more than ready to rise to the challenge.

Favourite Game of the Season
We started the season well and I think the most memorable game for me was the win at home over Ipswich Town in August. They came to Gresty Road as one of the teams well fancied for the play-offs, and obviously they are a big club, but I thought we did well that day and it was a great result for us.

Worst Game of the Season
It was another game early in the season but this time we didn't do so well against West Ham. It was a big game against a team coming down from the Premier League but with 25 minutes gone we'd given it away by conceding three goals. It was a tough night for all of us.

Best Ground
There's been a few good ones in this Division but Derby County's Pride Park Ground was excellent with great facilities.

Game Looking Forward to
I am excited about playing Wolves at Molineux. I was born in Wolverhampton and still live there and most of my mates are big Wolves fans. It would be fantastic to win there.

Aspirations for Next Season
I have got to start becoming more of a regular in the first team this season. It is important to me to be holding down a regular starting place like I did at the beginning of last season.

Toughest Opponent
For me it was Paul Merson when we played Walsall at home. Although we won the game and they didn't score, I still thought he was pure class when he had the ball at his feet.

Anthony Tonkin

The former Yeovil Town and Stockport County full-back joined Crewe Alexandra in August 2003 after a prolonged chase for his signature. With then Stockport County boss Carlton Palmer reluctant to sell the Cornwall-born left-footer, Tonkin was forced into handing in a written transfer request before being allowed to join us for a fee rising to £175,000 depending on appearances.

Having been a keen admirer from his Yeovil days, Dario Gradi was eager to bring Tonkin to the Alexandra Stadium as the possible long-term replacement for former stalwart Shaun Smith. His arrival would also allow the manager to use David Vaughan in his natural position on the left hand side of midfield. The young Welshman is so committed to the Crewe cause that he has willingly accepted being played out of his preferred position for much of his career, but the arrival of Tonks should alter that.

That remains the long-term plan with Tonkin hoping to be involved in more games than he was last season. It took him a while to settle into the defensive system at Crewe, with both Dario and then his short-term replacement Neil Baker using him sparingly as a substitute, so he could take the step up to the First Division more gradually. He made his debut as a second-half substitute at Rotherham in September before starting against West Ham three days later.

With a sudden burst of speed and agility, Tonkin demonstrated throughout the season that he has the qualities to be a reliable and committed defender, as well as an asset going forward.

Tonkin continued to be in-and-out of the side for much of the season with untimely injuries and dips in form seeing him make 27 appearances in all competitions. Last season was one of transition for the 24-year-old defender, but hard work on the training ground and in the gymnasium should pay dividends this coming season.

'It will be nice to get a full pre-season under my belt after what happened at Stockport last season! I think I've developed as a player since coming to Crewe and hopefully during the summer, I can eradicate some of the errors in my game and come back even stronger for the new campaign,' says Tonks.

'From a personal point of view my first year at Crewe went better than expected. I played more games than I thought I would and developed my game as a consequence.

'I did have some indifferent games and was left out of the side but I think that worked in my favour as it only increased my motivational levels to try and get back into the side.'

The left back adds: 'I'm looking forward to the new season and hopefully I can use the advantage of having a pre-season to establish myself in the side when we kick off again in August because I got an injury at the wrong time at the end of the season and wasn't involved in the run-in as much as I would liked.'

To his credit, Tonkin was making considerable progress until he sustained an ankle injury in training over the Easter weekend, which effectively ruled him out for the next four crucial matches against Coventry, Reading, Crystal Palace and Sunderland. He finished the season with a brief substitute appearance against Norwich on the final day and rather harshly conceded the late penalty, which commended us to a 3–1 defeat against the champions.

A former England semi-professional during his days with Yeovil, one of the reasons Tonkin decided to come to Crewe Alexandra was to learn and improve as a player under the coaching of Dario Gradi and his staff. Eager to develop as a player, you can rest assured that the best is yet to come from the club's first choice left-back.

Favourite Game of the Season
That would be Sunderland at home when we won 3–0. We had a bit of luck in the first half to keep it goalless, but we deservedly won the game for our second-half performance.

Worst Game of the Season
Away at Cardiff when we lost 3–0 back in October.

Best Ground
Ipswich Town.

Game Looking Forward to
I am looking forward to going to newly promoted Plymouth because a few of my family can attend the game there.

Aspirations for Next Season
My aim is to establish myself in the team and improve on what I achieved last season.

Toughest Opponent
Gary Teale of Wigan and Jobi McAnuff of West Ham. They were both quick and always run at you when they get the opportunity.

Justin Cochrane

When Justin Cochrane arrived from non-league Hayes FC for a £50,000 fee in July, almost no one would have predicted the impact he would have in the Alex's first season back in the First Division.

After playing several friendlies for the reserves as a trialist, the young Londoner was invited to join the Alex for pre-season training by assistant manager Neil Baker, and quickly made an impression. An injury to Neil Sorvel then handed Justin a further chance to impress Dario Gradi when he was invited to join the rest of the first-team squad as Sorvs's late replacement on a pre-season training camp in Portugal.

What Dario saw during that week in the Algarve was a talented, energetic, tough tackling and wholly committed player who he immediately wanted to add to his squad. Although the midfield wasn't a position the Alex boss had considered strengthening at the end of the 2002–03 season, Cochrane's performances earned him a two-year contract, which the Hackney-born player signed just prior to our pre-season testimonial game against Liverpool.

It was an amazing turnaround in the career of Cochrane, who just 12 months earlier had been told he had no future at Queens Park Rangers, the club he had played for as a youngster. After captaining the R's Youth Team, Justin finally got his first team chance against Stockport County. Unfortunately things went badly wrong on that April afternoon at Loftus Road when, just 17 minutes after coming on as a substitute, Cochrane was harshly sent off for a tackle on Shefki Kuqi. He never played for QPR again and was released the following season.

Unlike so many young players though, the level-headed Cochrane was quickly back in football as he sought to rebuild his career by dropping into the Ryman League with Hayes. After scoring on his debut he enjoyed a superb season in the part-time game and was soon spotted after introducing himself to Crewe scout Bill Berry (who sadly passed away this summer) at a game against St Albans. Despite being suspended that day, Bill monitored Justin's progress and had no hesitation in recommending him to Neil Baker – and thank goodness he did, especially with Chelsea reported to be interested in taking him to Stamford Bridge.

After penning his contract, Cochrane's debut in front of the home fans came at Gresty Road when the Alex played Everton. On a sunny evening he stunned supporters in a 2–0 victory over the Toffeemen by comfortably walking away with the Man-of-the-Match award.

His robust display had quickly won over the home faithful by covering every blade of grass for the Alex cause and matching up comfortably against the likes of full internationals Thomas Gravesen and Lee Carsley. After being substituted near the end of the match he looked slightly shell-shocked when the whole stadium rose to its feet to applaud him off the pitch and looked even more confused when he received rapturous applause from the Air Products stand as he warmed down on the touchline!

His displays in the rest of the pre-season programme were just a taster for what was to come when the season proper began. Cochrane starred in Crewe's midfield during the early games of the campaign and was particularly influential when Dave Brammer was absent with a pelvic injury. Unfortunately, a one-match ban ended his ever-present record when Telford United visited Gresty Road in the FA Cup, and then a pulled hamstring a week later against Wimbledon meant a spell on the sidelines.

Justin honestly admitted in the summer: 'This coming season I just want to get back playing the way I did at the beginning of last season. I had the hamstring injury and then I thought I was poor for a few games after that.

But I have come from playing non-league football to playing over 30 games so I think I got used to the pace of league football.

'Now the aim is to keep on improving and to try and get into the team and stay there because the competition for places here is excellent.

The likeable Londoner added: 'I am not interested in using the fact I came from non-league as an excuse as I have played enough games to have learned to adapt to what is needed at this level.

'Everybody knows how good a coach Dario is and how he can teach you and improve you as a player. He has a great history of doing that down the years and I think he has benefited me because I have definitely improved. There are still areas of my game that need more improvement but hopefully, the longer I stay with Dario then the better player I can become.'

Justin was soon back to his best towards the end of the season and although he struggled to displace the fit-again Brammer he deservedly picked up BBC Radio Stoke's 'Newcomer of the Year' award at the annual presentation dinner to cap an awesome first season for the Railwaymen.

Favourite Game of the Season

I enjoyed the home win over Stoke City. It was great to win that game and it was an important win as well with them being our local rivals. The fans were really terrific that night as well. The place was buzzing and it really made a difference to the players.

Worst Game of the Season

West Bromwich Albion at home. It was on Sky and we lost 2–1 but I thought my own personal performance was minging.

Best Ground

Upton Park, West Ham was a great stadium and a very good place to play.

Game Looking Forward to

I have to say my former club Queens Park Rangers who are coming up from the Second Division. It will be good to play at Loftus Road against them having spent so much time there as a youngster.

Aspirations for Next Season

I need to keep improving my all round game, but one thing I really want to do is score a few goals. The lads have tagged me 'John Jensen', the former Arsenal player, and I don't want that to last. I scored quite a few goals for Hayes before I signed for the Alex so I know I can get goals.

Toughest Opponent

When we played at Sheffield United before Christmas Stuart McCall really stood out as the best player on the pitch. He may be nearing 40 but he showed me how to play central midfield that day.

B.B.C. Radio Stoke
Newcomer of the Season
2003-04

Justin Cochrane

Billy Jones

One of the highlights of the 2003–04 season was the emergence of youngster Billy Jones. The England Youth international produced performances that belied his age and only confirmed what everyone had been thinking for a long time – Crewe have unearthed another talented youngster, who can go as far as he wants in the game.

Recommended to the club by former defender Dave Walton, the Shrewsbury-born Jones first came to prominence when as a mere 15-year-old he made a brief appearance against Macclesfield Town in a pre-season friendly. Dario only threw him on with five minutes to go at Moss Rose because he had genuinely forgotten that he had named the promising defender on the bench! It wasn't long though before Jones was making his mark in the Academy, in the Youth Team and on the international stage as captain of the England Under-16s.

Although trying to provide Rooney-esque protection to his talented 16-year-old, the urge to give Billy Jones his first team bow came as early as October in what was Dario Gradi's first game back from his heart valve replacement. Ironically, the opponents that day were Walton's new club Derby County and he must have felt immense pride when Jones replaced Justin Cochrane in the dying minutes.

When deployed in either defence or midfield, Jones did both jobs equally well and was nothing short of a revelation in his first season at senior level. Wholly at ease with either foot, the youngster possesses supreme authority for someone so young and not surprisingly the Crewe supporters are anxious for the club to hold on to him as long as possible.

Billy revealed in the close season: 'I was really happy with the way things went last season and it was fantastic to find myself in the team and playing First Division football. I think I did quite well although it was a bit of a rollercoaster ride which I expected it to be. I thought some games were better than others because it's a tough league to play in, but overall I was happy with way things went during my first season.

'It was surprising to play so many games in the first team because when I came into the side Dario told me that he wasn't going to play me in two consecutive games. However we had so many injuries at that time it meant that I stayed in the team and ended up playing more than everyone expected.

'I played quite a few positions but I think I enjoyed playing at right-back the most. I'm not really bothered where I play though as long as I am in the team and I hope that this coming season I can continue being in the starting line up and that we can improve on last year's finishing position.'

Although not particularly tall, Billy has a good spring and is strong in the air, which saw him most notably cope with the threat of former player Ashley Ward last season. Deceptively quick, Billy has more than enough pace to cover the ground and his upper-body strength has allowed him to comfortably handle the rigours of First Division football.

He deservedly won Dario Gradi's Young Player of the Year Award in May after making such a profound impact. The classy youngster propelled himself into the public spotlight with our Goal of the Season against Wigan in December. One straight off the training ground, Jones volleyed home a Kenny Lunt corner from 20 yards to leave everyone who witnessed it in total awe of his technical prowess.

On his international progress, Billy said: 'Internationally I was most pleased with my call up for the England Under-19s, which is two years ahead of my age group. That makes me think that I am doing something right and to be involved in the same team as players such as James Milner, who have Premiership experience, was an excellent experience.'

Unquestionably, Billy Jones has a very bright future in the game and hopefully he will become the linchpin of the Crewe defence in the next few years. As always, Dario Gradi will monitor his fitness with a sharp eye and like last season at the first sight of any fatigue he will be rested. You seem to forget that he is still only 17.

Favourite Game of the Season
It has to be the game in which I scored my goal at home to Wigan.

Worst Game of the Season
When we lost to Telford in the FA Cup. It was very disappointing to go out like that plus I am from Shrewsbury so I got some stick for that.

Favourite Away Ground
The Stadium of Light.

Fixture Most Looking Forward to
I'm looking forward to playing at Elland Road when we play Leeds away.

Aspirations for Next Season
To improve our position in the table from last season.

Toughest Player Faced Last Season
Eddie Lewis from Preston. I thought he was a good player and he roughed me up a bit as well!

Lee Bell

What began as a season of great promise for Lee Bell ended with him making just three substitute appearances for Crewe Alexandra. Those brief performances against Wimbledon, Ipswich and Coventry early on in the campaign totalled just 41 minutes on the pitch, before the local lad was agreeing to join Shrewsbury Town on a season-long loan deal. Things didn't go according to plan at Gay Meadow, with the highly competitive midfielder making just one start for Jimmy Quinn's side away at Scarborough.

Bell returned to Crewe prematurely in early January and to his credit worked hard to try and advance up the midfield pecking order. He was even named as an unused substitute for the games against Millwall and Walsall – but he failed to add to his 25 first team appearances.

This coming season is a huge one for many of the younger players at the club, and Bell will have to start reproducing the form that saw him score that spectacular goal against Colchester United and claim the Man-of-the-Match Award for the visit of Wycombe Wanderers during our promotion season.

Luke Varney

Despite missing three months of the campaign with a troublesome shoulder problem, last season will always be a memorable one for Luke Varney. Not only did he convince everyone that he has a chance of making an impact in the professional game, but his injury lay-off to correct a dislocation has seen him improve many aspects of his game including his strength, reading of the game and pace.

The speed merchant who signed from Quorn FC will fondly recall his brief substitute appearance against his hometown club Leicester City in the Carling Cup and his first-ever league goal away at Crystal Palace on his full league debut.

Overall, Varney made 10 first-team appearances, including six starts against the likes of West Brom, Wigan and Preston. Just as it looked as though he was beginning to find his feet after a consistent run of games, he was injured during our FA Cup exit to Telford United and did not return to full time training until April.

A few outings for the 'reserves' had Dario Gradi marvelling over his improvement and obvious potential. The pre-season will determine just how close he is to a first-team return. Maybe he will come through and provide suitable cover for the similarly quick Steve Jones.

Chris McCready

Chris McCready will be hoping for an injury free season after enduring more than his fair share of problems over the last couple of years. A succession of niggling muscle injuries combined to stall his progression last season – but fitness permitting the Chester-based defender could play a vital role in this coming campaign, especially if Dario elects to operate with the new wing-back formation he briefly used in the final game against Norwich City. When he does play, McCready is an accomplished defender who has never let the side down whether he operates as full-back or as central defender.

He certainly impressed during his 23 appearances last season, claiming the Man-of-the-Match Award for his display against Cardiff City in mid-March. He was making steady progress until he suffered a thigh strain and with a new contract then yet to be resolved, it was a worrying time for the assured 22-year-old.

An extension to his contract has been offered and looks likely to be accepted by a player who could become more than just a bit-part player in 2004/05. Chris has now made 33 career appearances since making his league debut at Millwall back in December 2001.

James Robinson

After making his first team debut during the Alex's promotion season in 2002/03 as a substitute against Peterborough United, James Robinson will be happy to have added another 10 appearances last season – but will be hoping to cement a more regular place this coming term.

Robinson signed a three-year contract with the club prior to the start of last term and was rewarded for his hard work through the summer with his full debut in the opening game of the season at Wimbledon. With Dean Ashton out through injury the 21-year-old Liverpudlian partnered Steve Jones up front at Selhurst Park, but on a sweltering afternoon had little opportunity to shine against Stuart Murdoch's side.

However he continued his hard work on the training pitches and was used in a variety of roles, predominantly across the midfield, as he made a further nine appearances as a substitute throughout the season.

He was perhaps unfortunate not to be handed another start, as Dario Gradi's side battled to avoid relegation, as he always made an impression when coming off the bench.

Perhaps Robinson's greatest memory of the season though will have come in the ill-fated trip to Portman Road, where the Alex lost 6–4 in an incredible match.

With the 'Tractor Boys' leading 5–3 in the dying minutes, he latched onto a Billy Jones flick on and buried a shot under goalkeeper Kelvin Davies to score his first senior goal in professional football.

With two years to run on his current deal Robinson, who originally signed professionally with the club in January 2001 after emerging through the Academy set up, will recognise that this coming campaign is a big one and he needs to be collecting more starts in the first team if his dream of a regular place at Crewe Alexandra is to be realised.

Paul Edwards

Derby-born Paul Edwards still has to convince the club's coaching staff that he is the youngster most likely to fill the void if Dean Ashton was ever injured or transferred. This coming season could well be his last big chance to reassert himself as one of the club's main goal threats after he failed to score in any of his 11 appearances last season.

Granted, only three of those were actual starts – but for a player who scored so prolifically at Academy level he could well have opened his account against Leicester City or Millwall during the last campaign. His substitute appearance alongside fellow Academy graduate James Robinson during the 6–4 defeat at Ipswich Town was certainly encouraging as Dario seeks for those suitable replacements for his regular front two.

Edwards is a hard-working forward, who wins his fair share of aerial battles and given a chance he can usually tuck it away with calm authority. It just hasn't happened for him yet at first-team level and maybe that elusive first goal will give him the extra confidence he needs to finally make that breakthrough.

I'm sure he will be thrown into the fray at some point during the pre-season and forthcoming season, it's just a question of whether Paul Edwards can grab that chance with both hands.

Stuart Tomlinson

Stuart Tomlinson began his football career as an outfield player, but has developed into one of the Club's most promising young goalkeepers for many years. Although the club's envied Academy has produced talented players, it has struggled to find a goalkeeper of any real note. Kevin Welsby was probably the nearest to making a breakthrough before he was released and found himself performing at non-league level.

Chester-born Tomlinson has a decent chance of breaking that particular mould, having impressed at Academy level and during his two brief substitute outings at Oldham and West Ham. He performed admirably at Oldham during our promotion season having replaced the injured Danny Milosevic on 51 minutes and was called upon again to take the place of number one Clayton Ince when he strained a thigh at West Ham last season.

Tomlinson could be one for the future and learning from the likes of Clayton Ince and Ben Williams will only enhance his chances of making that huge step up to first-team level.

Michael Higdon

Michael Higdon was one of 12 players to be signed to a professional contract in January 2001 following his excellent displays for the Academy youngsters and the Youth Cup side. Higdon and Dean Ashton are the younger ones of that record-breaking group and it certainly took the Liverpool-born youngster more time to make that decisive breakthrough into the first-team squad. He achieved that and more last season and could yet prove to be the answer to the manager's centre-forward problems.

Higdon possesses the aerial ability and eye for goal that could yet see him converted into a reliable replacement for Dean Ashton.

Having only made his debut as a late substitute in the 3–1 victory at Crystal Palace, the normally patient Crewe supporters were rather unfair to him on his full home debut against Wigan just a couple of weeks later and then again against Telford United in the FA Cup. To be fair, Higdon's shooting was wayward on some occasions during those games, but he showed incredible mental strength to continue to shoot from distance and make forward runs into the box.

'The Don' got his just rewards with his first senior goal against Coventry City on Easter Monday, which set us on the way to a valuable three points. The manager showed tremendous faith in the youngster by starting him up front with his close pal Michael Symes. It paid off in remarkable fashion with Crewe winning 3–1 and both lads were on target in one of the most memorable days of the campaign. He finished the season with 11 appearances to his name and he will be looking to add to that total during this forthcoming season.

Gary Roberts

Although Billy Jones may have taken all the headlines this season as the next 'player from the Crewe Alexandra production line', his 17-year-old team-mate Gary Roberts is not far behind in the opinion of Dario Gradi.

The combative midfield playmaker isn't quite as physically advanced as Jones, but he too made his first team debut last season and is expected to play a big part in the future of the football club. Roberts was handed his debut as a substitute in the 3–1 home win over Burnley and also featured in the 1–0 triumph over Wimbledon in January.

It was at youth team level where he really starred though, playing a crucial role in the run to the FA Youth Cup Semi-Finals despite missing a couple of rounds due to a knee injury sustained at Cirencester Town.

Roberts also starred on the international stage with England, representing his country at Under-16 level and also at the UEFA European Under-17 Championships in France during the month of May.

With competition fierce for a berth in Crewe's midfield, Roberts may have to wait until he has grown a little more before he begins to compete for a regular place in Dario's side, but the youngster has certainly done enough over the past 12 months to suggest he is another potential star of the future. And bearing in mind he only starts the second year of his scholarship this season, he has plenty of time on his side.

Youth Cup Action

Milk Cup Results 2003

Date	Opponents		Scorers
19 July 03	NK Factor (Slovenia)	3-0	Howard, Carrington, Jones
21 July 03	County Londonderry	1-0	Maynard
22 July 03	Botafogo (Brazil)	1-1	Howard
23 July 03	U.Catolica (Chile) QF	0-0	Lost 5-4 on pens
24 July 03	Leeds United (Play Off)	1-2	Bond
25 July 03	Botafogo (Brazil) (7th/8th Play Off)	3-1	Bond (2), Holroyd

FA Youth Cup Results 2003/04

Date	Opponents			Scorers
2 December 03	Brentford	1-0		Roberts
4 February 04	Cirencester Town	1-1	aet	Kerr (Won 6-5 on pens)
25 February 04	Sunderland	2-1	aet	Kerr, Wilson (pen)
3 March 04	Swindon Town (QF)	3-0		Howard, Maynard, Wilson
18 March 04	Middlesbrough (SF1)	0-2		
7 March 04	Middlesbrough (SF2)	0-1		

Crewe's Welsh Youth international Owain fon Williams keeps guard against Brentford.

The Crewe players celebrate Nicky Maynard's goal against Swindon Town

England Under-19 international Kyle Wilson celebrates the third goal against Swindon.

FA Premier Academy League – Under-17 Results 2003/04

August

| Saturday 23 | Home | Watford | 5-0 | Roberts (2), Dugdale, Matthews, Kerr |
| Saturday 30 | Away | Leicester City | 3-4 | Hendricks, Maynard, Roberts |

September

Saturday 6	Home	Leeds United	0-1	
Saturday 13	Away	Wolves	0-1	
Saturday 20	Home	Middlesbrough	4-0	Maynard, Collymore, Jones, Roberts (pen)
Saturday 27	Home	Nottingham Forest	1-1	Carrington

October

Saturday 4	Away	Derby County	2-1	Hogg (2)
Saturday 11	Away	Sheffield United	0-2	
Saturday 18	Home	Wolves	1-2	Mannion
Saturday 25	Away	Leeds United	0-1	

November

Saturday 1	Away	Nottingham Forest	1-1	Flynn
Saturday 8	Home	Manchester City	1-3	Dillon
Saturday 15	Home	Blackburn Rovers	4-5	Roberts (3), Matthews
Saturday 22	Away	Liverpool	1-2	Maynard

December

| Saturday 6 | Home | Manchester United | 1-1 | Maynard |
| Saturday 13 | Away | Everton | 2-2 | Flynn, Oates |

January

| Saturday 10 | Away | Blackburn Rovers | 1-5 | Matthews |
| Saturday 24 | Away | Manchester United | 0-0 | |

February

Saturday 14	Away	Manchester City	2-2	O'Connor, Oates
Saturday 21	Home	Blackburn Rovers	0-2	
Saturday 28	Away	Liverpool	0-5	

March

Saturday 6	Home	Derby County	4-3	Holroyd (2), Maynard, Collymore
Saturday 13	Home	Sheffield United	1-1	Maynard
Saturday 20	Away	Middlesbrough	8-7	Clements (2), Westwood (2), Lloyd, Brown, Calvert, Leitch-Smith
Monday 23	Away	Everton	0-3	
Saturday 27	Home	Liverpool	4-3	Warlow (3), Farquharson

FA Premier Academy League – Under-19 Results 2003/04

August

| Saturday 23 | Home | Watford | 2-2 | Bond, Wilson |
| Saturday 30 | Away | Leicester City | 3-2 | Howard, Wilson, Oates |

September

Saturday 6	Home	Huddersfield Town	3-0	Fletcher, Howard, Brown
Saturday 13	Away	Barnsley	4-1	Howard (2), Wilson (2)
Saturday 27	Away	Sunderland	2-2	Wilson, Lloyd

October

Saturday 4	Home	Sheffield Wed	2-2	Wilson, Howard
Saturday 11	Away	Bolton Wanderers	3-1	Wilson, McGowan, Fletcher
Saturday 18	Home	Blackburn Rovers	1-1	Wilson
Saturday 25	Away	Manchester United	2-4	Bond, Howard

November

Saturday 1	Home	Liverpool	1-1	Fletcher
Saturday 8	Home	Everton	0-0	
Friday 14	Away	Manchester City	1-3	Wilson
Saturday 22	Home	Stoke City	1-0	Wilson

December

| Saturday 0 | Away | Wolves | 1-2 | Wilson |

Winger Mark Carrington threads a through ball through the middle.

January

Saturday 10	Away	Liverpool	0-1	
Saturday 17	Away	Everton	1-1	O'Connor
Saturday 24	Home	Manchester City	2-1	Howard, Hawthorne

February

Saturday 7	Away	Stoke City	2-2	Fletcher, Brown
Saturday 14	Home	Wolves	1-1	Fletcher
Saturday 21	Away	Sheffield Wed	2-0	Bond, Fletcher
Saturday 28	Home	Bolton Wanderers	0-2	

March

Saturday 13	Home	Manchester United	1-0	own goal
Saturday 20	Home	Middlesbrough	1-0	Flynn
Saturday 27	Home	Nottingham Forest	2-1	Wilson, Hawthorne

April

Saturday 3	Away	Newcastle United	1-4	Howard
Wednesday 14	Home	Blackburn Rovers	1-2	Oates

The Crewe coaching staff watch Cavell Coo in action against Danish outfit Brondby.

Reaseheath Training Ground

All the Crewe players develop their physique in the state of the art gymnasium.

The indoor sports hall was a compulsory requirement as part of our Academy status.

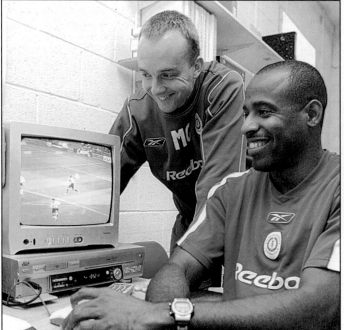

Kenny Lunt enjoys a laugh while undergoing his stretching exercises.

The players undergo video analysis after every game under the guidance of Mick Cort.

The facilities at Reaseheath are now of 'Premiership class'.

Steve Jones retains possession in a training 5-a-side match.

Mark Roberts intercepts a pass from David Wright, as Chris McCready and James Robinson wait for any loose ball.

Craig Hignett holds off a challenge from Anthony Tonkin.

Opposition Preview

Brighton & Hove Albion

Stadium & Address: Withdean Stadium
Tongdean Lane off
London Road
Brighton
BN1 1YR

Ticket Office Number: 01273 776992

Website: www.seagulls.co.uk

Ground Capacity: 6,973

Nickname: The Seagulls

Directions: M6 South to join M42. Leave M42 at junction 3(a) to join M40 (signposted London). Continue on M40 at junction 1(a) to join M25 (heading anti-clockwise). Leave M25 at junction 7 to join M23 (Signposted Brighton) Exit M23 at junction 11 and join A23 to Brighton. The ground is situated in Tongdean Lane just off A23 after Peacock Lane.

Nearest Train Station: Preston Park (10 minutes walk)

Car Parking: No parking near the stadium – take park and ride buses or walk

Last Season's Finishing Position: 4th (Second Division – promoted via play-offs)

Top Goalscorer: Leon Knight – 27

Ones to watch: Leon Knight, Guy Butters, Nathan Jones, Danny Cullip

Last season v the Alex: N/A

Burnley

Stadium & Address: Turf Moor
Harry Potts Way
Burnley
BB10 4BX

Ticket Office Number: 0870 443 1914

Website: www.burnleyfootballclub.com

Ground Capacity: 22,000

Nickname: The Clarets

Directions: M6 North to M62. Leave M62/M60 at junction 18 to join M66. At the end of the Motorway join A56 until you reach M65. Leave M65 at junction 10 to join A671 and then A682 into the Town Centre. Take first exit at roundabout (Gala Club) into Yorkshire Street. Follow through traffic signals into Harry Potts Way.

Nearest Train Station: Burnley Central (1½ miles)

Car Parking: Ormerod Road, adjacent to the Fire Station (2 minutes walk) and Fulledge Recreation Ground (2 mins walk)

Last Season's Finishing Position: 19th

Top Goalscorer: Robbie Blake – 22

Ones to watch: Robbie Blake, Richard Chaplow, Mohammed Camara, David May

Last Season v the Alex   Burnley   1-0 Crewe
                                Crewe   3-1 Burnley

Cardiff City

Stadium & Address: Ninian Park
Sloper Road
Cardiff
CF11 8SX

Ticket Office Number: 0845 345 1400

Website: www.cardiffcityfc.co.uk

Ground Capacity: 21,500

Nickname: The Bluebirds

Directions: M6 South to junction 8 and then join M5 South. Leave M5 at junction 8 and join M50. At end of Motorway join A40 and follow signs for M4. Leave M4 at junction 33 and follow Penarth (A4232) signs. After 6 miles take B4267 to Ninian Park.

Nearest Train Station: Cardiff Central

Car Parking: Leckwith Stadium Car Park (adjacent to ground)

Last Season's Finishing Position: 13th

Top Goalscorer: Robert Earnshaw – 26

Ones to watch: Danny Gabbidon, Robert Earnshaw, Richard Langley, Graham Kavanagh

Last Season v the Alex   Cardiff   3-0 Crewe
Crewe   0-1 Cardiff

Coventry City

Stadium & Address: Highfield Road Stadium
King Richard Street
Coventry
CV2 4FW

Ticket Office Number: 024 7623 4020

Website: www.ccfc.co.uk

Ground Capacity: 23,613

Nickname: The Sky Blues

Directions: M6 junction 2. Take the A4600 and follow signs for City Centre. Cross two roundabouts staying on A4600. The road bears left, take the right exit at the next roundabout and continue for 1 mile. Turn right into Swan Lane just after the bridge and the ground is directly ahead.

Nearest Train Station: Coventry (1 mile)

Car Parking: Street Parking only

Last Season's Finishing Position: 12th

Top Goalscorer: Gary McSheffrey – 12

Ones to watch: Graham Barrett, Gary McSheffrey, Andrew Whing, Calum Davenport

Last Season v the Alex   Coventry 2-0 Crewe
Crewe   3-1 Coventry

Derby County

Stadium & Address: Pride Park Stadium
Royal Way
Pride Park
Derby
DE24 8XL

Ticket Office Number: 0870 444 1884

Website: www.dcfc.co.uk

Ground Capacity: 33,597

Nickname: The Rams

Directions: Exit M1 at junction 25 and then follow the A52 towards the City Centre. Ground is then well signposted and follow signs until arriving at Pride Park.

Nearest Train Station: Derby Midland (1 mile)

Car Parking: Spaces for 1,200 cars at the ground (permit holders only)

Last Season's Finishing Position: 20th

Top Goalscorer: Ian Taylor – 12

Ones to watch: Lee Holmes, Paul Peschisolido, Tom Huddlestone, Marco Reich

Last season v the Alex: Derby   0-0 Crewe
Crewe   3-0 Derby

Gillingham

Stadium & Address: Priestfield Stadium
Redfern Avenue
Gillingham
ME7 4DD

Ticket Office Number: 01634 300000

Website: www.gillinghamfootballclub.com

Ground Capacity: 10,992

Nickname: The Gills

Directions: M6 South to M1. M1 South to junction 6a and join M25 (Signposted Stansted Airport, M11). Continue clockwise on M25 until junction 2 and join A2. Continue on A2 and join M2. Leave M2 at junction 4 and follow the link road (dual carriageway) B278 to the 3rd roundabout. Turn left onto A2 and go across roundabout to traffic lights. Turn right into Woodlands Road after the traffic light. Ground is ½ mile on the left.

Nearest Train Station: Gillingham

Car Parking: Street Parking only

Last Season's Finishing Position 21st

Top Goalscorer: Patrick Agyemang – 6
Paul Shaw – 6
Danny Spiller – 6
Mamady Sidibe – 6

Ones to watch: Nyron Nosworthy, Patrick Agyemang, Danny Spiller, Andy Hessenthaler

Last season v the Alex: Gillingham 2-0 Crewe
Crewe   1-1 Gillingham

Ipswich Town

Stadium & Address:	Portman Road Ipswich, IP1 2DA
Ticket Office Number:	01473 400555
Website:	www.itfc.co.uk
Ground Capacity:	30,326
Nickname:	The Tractor Boys

Directions: M6 South to end of motorway and then join A14. Stay on A14 until junction 53 and then join A1156. After 2 miles join A1214 (Signposted Colchester) and then at junction with A137 (AA Service Centre) join A137. Ground is on left.

Nearest Train Station: Ipswich (5 minutes walk)

Car Parking: Portman Road and Sir Alf Ramsey Car Parks

Last Season's Finishing Position: 5th

Top Goalscorer: Darren Bent – 16

Ones to watch: Tommy Miller, Jason De Vos, Shefqi Kuqi, Jim Magilton.

Last season v the Alex: Ipswich 6-4 Crewe
Crewe 1-0 Ipswich

Leeds United

Stadium & Address:	Elland Road Leeds LS11 0ES
Ticket Office Number:	0845 121 1992
Website:	www.leedsunited.com
Ground Capacity:	40,232
Nickname:	United or the Whites

Directions: Take M62 to junction 27 and join M621. Leave M621 at junction 2 and leave roundabout onto A643 into Elland Road.

Nearest Train Station: Leeds City (1½ miles)

Car Parking: Large car parks adjacent to the stadium

Last Season's Finishing Position: 19th Premier League

Top Goalscorer: Mark Viduka – 12

Ones to watch: James Milner, Matthew Kilgallon, Frazer Richardson, Scott Carson

Last Season v the Alex: N/A

Leicester City

Stadium & Address:	The Walkers Stadium
	Filbert Way
	Leicester
	LE2 7FL
Ticket Office Number:	(0870) 0406000
Website:	www.lcfc.co.uk
Ground Capacity:	32,500
Nickname:	The Foxes

Directions: Exit M1 at junction 21 and take A5460. Turn right ½ mile after the Railway Bridge into Upperton Road and then right into Filbert Way.

Nearest Train Station: St Margaret's (1 Mile from Ground)

Car Parking: NCP Car Park (5 minutes walk)

Last Season's Finishing Position: 18th Premier League

Top Goalscorer: Paul Dickov – 14

Ones to watch: James Scowcroft, Lilian Nalis, Jordan Stewart, Ian Walker

Last season v the Alex: Leicester 1-0 Crewe (Carling Cup)

Millwall

Stadium & Address:	The New Den
	Zampa Road
	London
	SE16 3LN
Ticket Office Number:	0870 403 3357
Website:	www.millwallfc.co.uk
Ground Capacity:	20,146
Nickname:	The Lions

Directions: Follow City signs from the M1 then signs for Shoreditch and Whitechapel. Follow Ring Road signs for Dover, cross over Tower Bridge and after 1 mile take 1st exit at the roundabout onto the A2. From Elephant and Castle take the A2 (New Kent Road) into Old Kent Road and turn left after 4 miles at Canterbury Arms pub into Ilderton Road to Zampa Road.

Nearest Train Station: New Cross Gate / South Bermondsey (½ mile)

Car Parking: Adjacent to the ground

Last Season's Finishing Position: 10th

Top Goalscorer: Tim Cahill – 12

Ones to watch: Paul Ifil, Daniele Dichio, Dennis Wise, Darren Ward

Last season v the Alex: Millwall 1-1 Crewe
Crewe 1-2 Millwall

Nottingham Forest

Stadium & Address: City Ground
Nottingham
NG2 5FJ

Ticket Office Number: 0871 226 1980

Website: www.nottinghamforest.co.uk

Ground Capacity: 30,602

Nickname: The Reds

Directions: A500 then A50 to M1 junction 24. Then follow signs for Nottingham (South) to Trent Bridge. Turn Right into Radcliffe Road then left into Colwick Road for the ground.

Nearest Train Station: Nottingham Midland (½ mile)

Car Parking: East Car Park (300 spaces) and street parking

Last Season's Finishing Position: 14th

Top Goalscorer: Andy Reid – 13

Ones to watch: David Johnson, Michael Dawson, Gareth Williams, Gareth Taylor.

Last season v the Alex: Forest 2-0 Crewe
Crewe 3-1 Forest

Plymouth Argyle

Stadium & Address: Home Park
Plymouth
PL2 3DQ

Ticket Office Number: 01752 606167

Website: www.pafc.co.uk

Ground Capacity: 20,134

Nickname: The Pilgrims

Directions: M6 South to junction 8 and then join M5. Leave M5 at junction 31 and then join A38. Continue on A38 to A386 (Tavistock Road). Branch left following signs for Plymouth and continue for 1½ miles to ground.

Nearest Train Station: Plymouth North Road

Car Parking: Car park for 1000 cars is adjacent to ground

Last Season's Finishing Position: Champions (Second Division)

Top Goalscorer: David Friio – 15

Ones to watch: Paul Wotton, David Friio, Paul Connolly, Marino Keith.

Last season v the Alex: N/A

Preston North End

Stadium & Address:	Deepdale Preston PR1 6RU
Ticket Office Number:	0870 442 1966
Website:	www.pne.com
Ground Capacity:	22,226
Nickname:	The Lilywhites

Directions: Exit M6 at junction 31 and follow Preston signs (A59). Take 2nd exit at the roundabout (1 mile) into Blackpool Road. Turn left after 1½ miles into Deepdale.

Nearest Train Station: Preston (2 miles)

Car Parking: Sir Tom Finney car park, Moor Park and Deepdale Primary School

Last Season's Finishing Position: 15th

Top Goalscorer: Ricardo Fuller – 19

Ones to watch: David Healy, Ricardo Fuller, Graham Alexander, Chris Lucketti.

Last season v the Alex: Preston 0-0 Crewe
Crewe 2-1 Preston

Queens Park Rangers

Stadium & Address:	Loftus Road South Africa Road London W12 7PA
Ticket Office Number:	0870 112 1967
Website:	www.qpr.co.uk
Ground Capacity:	18,400
Nickname:	Rangers or the R's

Directions: M6 South to M1 South until end of Motorway. Then take the North Circular Road for Neasden. Go left after ½ mile (A404) following signs for Harlesden, Hammersmith. Go past White City Stadium and right into White City Road then left into South Africa Road.

Nearest Train Station: Shepherd's Bush

Car Parking: Street parking only

Last Season's Finishing Position: 2nd (Second Division)

Top Goalscorer: Kevin Gallen – 17

Ones to watch: Marcus Bignot, Paul Furlong, Kevin Gallen, Danny Shittu.

Last season v the Alex: N/A

Reading

Stadium & Address: Madejski Stadium
Reading
Berkshire
RG2 OFL

Ticket Office Number: 0118 968 1000

Website: www.readingfc.co.uk

Ground Capacity: 24,084

Nickname: The Royals

Directions: M6 South to join M42 and then M40. Leave M40 at junction 4 and join A404. Continue on A404 until you join M4. Join M4 and leave at junction 11 and the Stadium is situated just off this junction.

Nearest Train Station: Reading Central

Car Parking: 1800 spaces available at Ground with 2000 more nearby

Last Season's Finishing Positions 9th

Top Goalscorer: Shaun Goater – 14

Ones to watch: Dave Kitson, Nicky Forster, Steven Sidwell, Glen Little.

Last season v the Alex: Reading 1-1 Crewe
Crewe 1-0 Reading

Rotherham United

Stadium & Address: Millmoor Stadium
Rotherham
S60 1HR

Ticket Office Number: 01709 309440

Website: www.themillers.co.uk

Ground Capacity: 11,499

Nickname: The Millers

Directions: Exit M1 at junction 34 and follow Rotherham (A6109 signs to traffic lights and turn right. The ground is ½ mile on the right over the Railway Bridge.

Nearest Train Station: Rotherham Central (½ mile)

Car Parking: Kimberworth Road and Main Street car parks

Last Season's Finishing Position: 17th

Top Goalscorer: Martin Butler – 15

Ones to watch: Martin Butler, Andy Monkhouse, Jody Morris, John Mullin.

Last season v the Alex: Rotherham 0-2 Crewe
Crewe 0-0 Rotherham

Sheffield United

Stadium & Address: Bramall Lane
Sheffield
S2 4SU

Ticket Office Number: 0870 787 1799

Website: www.sufc.co.uk

Ground Capacity: 30,935

Nickname: The Blades

Directions: Take A54 (Through Congleton and Buxton) into Sheffield and take the 4th exit at the roundabout into Upper Hanover Street. At the 2nd roundabout take 3rd exit into Bramall Lane.

Nearest Train Station: Sheffield Midland (1 mile)

Car Parking: Street parking only

Last Season's Finishing Position: 8th

Top Goalscorer: Jack Lester – 15

Ones to watch: Michael Tonge, Phil Jagielka, Andy Gray, Stuart McCall.

Last season v the Alex: Sheff Utd   2-0   Crewe
Crewe   0-1   Sheff Utd

Stoke City

Stadium & Address: Britannia Stadium
Stanley Matthews Way
Stoke-on-Trent
ST4 4EG

Ticket Office Number: 01782 592204

Website: www.stokecity.co.uk

Ground Capacity: 28,218

Nickname: The Potters

Directions: Take the A500 out of Crewe and then join A50 at 'Sideway Junction'. Branch Left Signposted Uttoxter. At Heron Cross junction Branch Left and at Roundabout take 4th exit and return to A50 (U-turn). Britannia Stadium is on left.

Nearest Train Station: Stoke-on-Trent (1½ miles)

Car Parking: At the ground (bookings necessary). Also various car parks within a 10 minute walk.

Last Season's Finishing Position: 11th

Top Goalscorer: Gifton Noel-Williams – 10
Ade Akinbiyi – 10

Ones to watch: John Halls, Ade Akinbiyi, Kris Commons, Gifton Noel-Williams.

Last season v the Alex: Stoke   1-1   Crewe
Crewe   2-0   Stoke

Sunderland

Stadium & Address: Stadium of Light
Sunderland
SR5 1SU

Ticket Office Number: 0191 551 5151

Website: www.safc.com

Ground Capacity: 48,300

Nickname: The Black Cats

Directions: M1 then A1 and exit the A1 at the A690 Durham/Sunderland exit. After approximately 4 miles turn left onto the A19 (signposted Tyne Tunnel). Keep in the left hand lane and take the slip road (signposted Washington/Sunderland) onto the bridge over the River Wear. Turn right onto A1231 (signposted Washington/Sunderland) and stay on this road going straight across four roundabouts into Sunderland. Continue straight through two sets of traffic lights and the Stadium is on the right after 1 mile.

Nearest Train Station: Sunderland (1 mile)

Car Parking: Spaces for 1,100 cars (reserved)

Last Season's Finishing Position: 3rd

Top Goalscorer: Kevin Kyle – 16
Marcus Stewart – 16

Ones to watch: Jeff Whitley, Mart Poom, Kevin Kyle, Tommy Smith.

Last Season v the Alex Sunderland 1-1 Crewe
Crewe 3-0 Sunderland

Watford

Stadium & Address: Vicarage Road Stadium
Watford
WD18 0ER

Ticket Office Number: 01923 496010

Website: www.watfordfc.com

Ground Capacity: 20,800

Nickname: The Hornets

Directions: Exit M1 at junction 5 and take the new road (A4008) towards Watford Town Centre. This will take you around the ring road and follow signs for Watford General Hospital. The ground is next to the hospital.

Nearest Train Station: Watford Junction or Watford Tube Station

Car Parking: Cardiff Road Car Park

Last Season's Finishing Position: 16th

Top Goalscorer: Scott Fitzgerald – 11

Ones to watch: Heidar Helgusson, Scott Fitzgerald, Hameur Bouazza, Paul Devlin.

Last season v the Alex: Watford 2-1 Crewe
Crewe 0-1 Watford

West Ham United

Stadium & Address: Boleyn Ground
Green Street
Upton Park
London, E13 9AZ

Ticket Office Number: 0870 112 2700

Website: www.whufc.com

Ground Capacity: 35,500

Nickname: The Hammers

Directions: From M1 take the North Circular (A406) to the A124 (East Ham) then along Barking Road for approximately 1½ miles until approaching traffic lights at the crossroads. Turn right into Green Street and the ground is on the right hand side.

Nearest Train Station: Barking

Car Parking: Street parking only

Last Season's Finishing Position: 4th

Top Goalscorer: Jermain Defoe – 15

Ones to watch: Jobi McAnuff, Nigel Reo-Coker, David Connolly, Marlon Harewood.

Last Season v the Alex West Ham 4-2 Crewe
Crewe 0-3 West Ham

Wigan Athletic

Stadium & Address: JJB Stadium
Robin Park
Newtown
Wigan, WN5 0UZ

Ticket Office Number: 0870 1122 552

Website: www.wiganathletic.tv

Ground Capacity: 25,000

Nickname: The Latics

Directions: Exit M6 at junction 25 and follow signs for Wigan (A49). After approx 2 miles a complex junction is reached. Keep in left hand lane (McDonalds on right). Turn left at traffic light filter lane into Robin Park road. Turn right at third set of traffic lights and follow road to Stadium.

Nearest Train Station: Wallgate and Wigan North Western (1 mile)

Car Parking: 2,500 spaces available at ground

Last Season's Finishing Position: 7th

Top Goalscorer: Nathan Ellington – 18

Ones to watch: Jason Roberts, Gary Teale, Nathan Ellington, Jimmy Bullard.

Last season v the Alex: Wigan 2-3 Crewe
Crewe 2-3 Wigan

Wolverhampton Wanderers

Stadium & Address:	Molineux Stadium Waterloo Road Wolverhampton WV1 4QR
Ticket Office Number:	0870 442 0123
Website:	www.wolves.co.uk
Ground Capacity:	29,400
Nickname:	Wolves

Directions: Exit M6 at junction 12 and take 3rd exit at Roundabout to join A5 (Wolverhampton). At next island turn left onto A449. After 6 miles A449 passes under M54, carry straight on and at 6th roundabout (Five Ways) take 3rd exit into Waterloo Road. Molineux is 1 mile straight ahead.

Nearest Train Station: Wolverhampton (½ mile)

Car Parking: Around West Park, Newhampton Road and rear of Stan Cullis Stand. Also in town centre (5 minute walk)

Last Season's Finishing Position: 20th Premier League

Top Goalscorer: Alex Rae – 8

Ones to watch: Carl Cort, Ioan Viroel Ganea, Henri Camara, Mark Kennedy.

Last season v the Alex: N/A

Supporters' Roll of Honour

Christopher James Smart

Andy "The Railwayman" Scoffin

David Mountford

Richard Fearn

Hannah Fearn

Sandra Foxley

Andrew McIntyre

Bolden Family

Andy Ferguson

Tony Brookes

Richard Cox

Anton Vucic

Jeff Lukomiak

Chris McGurn

Wilfred Ballard

Mick Earthman Gott

Mark Bowler

Junior

Charlotte Rodgers

Shaun Rodgers

James Hawkins

Keith Beale

John Dennel

Len McGarry

Vernon Poke

D.V. Jones

P. Hollinshead

Andrew Butterworth

David R Foster

Neil A Hancock

Kevin I Marsh

Brian Whittingham (WHIT)

Mr Anthony Corn

Lynne Tomlinson

Richard Barnett

Richard Kirkham

The 'Sorvel Legend' Banner Boys

Chris Thompson

Reg Platt

Steve Edwards

Ken Tomkinson

Steve Tomkinson

Ian Stevens

Chris Lawson

Nicole Lawson

Mike Redfern

Kevin P Hall

Julie Warren

Wilson Family

Callum Palin

Christina Bateman

Ben McClory

Jake Ferris

John Okey

Ian Bennett

Gordon Ellis

John Prentice

Dan Froskeland

Jennifer Woodbridge

The Greig Family

Alison Griffiths

Tracey Ball

Daniel Ball

Paul Robinson

Peter McGrath

David Lockyer

Mr E Sutton

Frank McN Jones

Thomas McN Jones

Robert Poole

James Poole

Jack Bloor

Mike Pullen

Chris Pullen

Mr Patrick McDermott

Len Knight

Derek Evanson

Bernard "Bert" Smith

Steven J Wakefield

Reidar Solberg (Norway)

Daniel Kinsey

Kenneth Moulton

J. Chris Holland

Nigel A Ball

Matthew Poke

Andrew Saunders

Chris Mason

Geoff Woollen

Luke Tinsley

Chris Harris

Philip Bowers

Dieter Thomas Bowers

James Johnston

Rob Woods

Deanna Cartlidge

Cliff Soames

Hannah Murphy

Lauren Murphy

Wilf Cope

Stephen Lea

The Wainwright Family

Lee Wood

Malcolm Bailey

Mark Jones (Pluggy)

Chris Stapleton

Karen Stapleton

Emma Porter

Tim Bush

Frank Lathem

Jim Forster

Richard Lowe

Philip Dodgson

Michelle Moore

Alan Morgan

Kevin J Bennison

Eddy O'Grady

John Iain Dunn

Edward Barnes

Jim Lacey

Pete Hollingsbee

John Arnold	John Rhodes
Andrew Warham	Nicola Jayne Steele
Elliot Bloor	James Byron Steele
Dave Platt	Janus Bodker (Denmark)
Matt Owen	Ross Carline
Emily Rose Normansell	Rick Flynn
Richard Taylor	Maz Ryan
Katie Bebbington	Alice Welch
Kevin Townsend	Tim Hardyment
Luke Simpson	John Gramstadt
Joe Cotton	Amelia Meakin-Bond
Jim Rowley	Eric McTurk
Lee Rowley	Graham Hallett
Adrian Booth	Charles Raymond
Brian James	Cliff Drake
Nigel Yoxall	Chris Murray
Trixie Carter	Daniel Stringer
Hornbrook Family	John Merrick
Hilary Robinson	Neil Hassall
Tim Robinson	Robert Proudlove
Howard Robinson	Paul Bader
Peter Robinson	The Parks
Matthew Egan	Greg Park
Andrew Siepen	Kyle McCann
Mike Hasprey	Richard P Lowe
Neil J Hassall	Will Cummins
Dennis Allcock	Linda Walker
Richard Clarke	Brian Copnall
Jake Ellison	Adam Copnall
Matt Herd	Alan Latham
Ben Geddes	Ellen Copnall
Hayden Whalley	Geoff Parsons
T Baker	Wilson Family

Amber Lea Godsell

Philip Hulse

Mr B L Thompson

Mike Skaife

David Gallagher

Tim Dutton

Robert Dutton

Kerri Williams

Peter Bull

Samantha Hassall

Matt Clarke

Jane Clarke

Sam Stockley

Robert Cox

Derek Cox

Ian McCaskill

Ron Bailey

Malcolm Bailey

Carl Siddall

Emma Highfield

Robert Highfield

Colin Higginson

Adam Williamson

Roy Clews

Dale Clews

Michael McGoldrick

Martin Caldwell

Darren Hollinshead

Brenda Wilkinson

Richard Howells

Thomas Owen-Evans

Zeke (Ray Jackson)

Kearns Family

Mr B Short

Liam James Norcup

Gary Norcup

Trevor Duckett

Chris Hughes

Alan Greene

Gail Tomlin

Paul Robert Haswell JNR

John Raynard

John Michael Lowndes

W.G. Oakes

Ian A Jones

Ernie Johnson

George McEvoy

Shaun Ellison

Arthur Sutton

John Sutton

Andrew Paul Rogers

John Roberts

Derick Edge

Tony Campion

John Campion

George Cooper

Ian Lowe

Gary Pearson

Peter Astley

Wendy Astley

Mike Cartwright

David Bale

Robert C Fox

Paulette Burns

Graham Chesters

Alexander Malam

Iain Martin	Rob Dulson
Hilda Davies	Jay Roberts
Neil Davies	Kay Turner
Martin Davies	Jim Hopping
Jane Davies	David Sutton
Mr Brian A Lucking	Karen Deborah Robinson
Andrew Groves	Kevin Charles Henson
George Groves	Anthony Conlon
Stephen Brown	Clowes Family
Shaun McCann	Gareth Roberts
Ian R W Lee	Steffan Whiteley
Cliff Brereton	Matthew Green
Eddie Littler	Lee Geary
Simon Lee	Baby Geary
Ian Garnett	John Geary
Richard Floy	John Latham
Gary Fagge	Rob Cradleton
James Talbot	Sinead Hamilton
Simon Talbot	Stuart Charles Harper
Adam Longhurst	The Affleck Family
Stephen Hatton	Paul Morris
James R Dodd	Michael Proudlove
George Arthur Griffiths	David Farrall
Julian Jarvis (Motley Crewe)	Neil Fearn
Lisa Brassington	Stephanie Fearn
Michael Blakemore	Thomas Dodd
Derek Owen	Les Lewis
Matthew Walker	Matt Doyle
Jim Lowndes	Tom Rhead
Ian Walker	Mike Lazenby
Michael Kosarew	Mr Andrew J Willavoys
Carey Robinson	Paul Rigby
Brent Robinson	Mick Matthews (Texas)

David Price

Alan Platt

Russell Platt

Darren Platt

Scott Kynnersley

Mr. Tanner

Wills Family

Tim Gallagher

Simon Edge

Adam Kay

Phil Benson

Richard Tomkinson

Tim Jones

Mark Taylor

In Memory Of David Davies

Michelle Harding

Philip Ashmore

Steve Lacey

Tim Mee

Wayne Jones

Michael Hughes

Simon Owens

Adam Brickwood

Michael Gresty

Martin 'Statto' Jenkins

John McVeigh

Carl Wood

Andy Williams

Amanda Butt

Paul Cooke

Karan Proudlove

Andrew Warham

Andrew Jodrell

Mrs Mary Clarke

Mr Anthony Tonkin

Lynne Sharratt

Keith Harding

Griffiths Family

Steve Churchill

Dan Churchill

Chris Moore

Linda Flevill

David Tomlinson

David Morris

Francis Hart

Lesley Sullivan

Steele Family

Phil Beckett

Hans Carlen

Justin Davies

Joan Marsland

Judette Maitland

John Arthur Taylor

Stuart McPhail

E Shankland